W9-BVL-245

CATS

CATS

The Nine Lives of Innovation

Stephen C. Lundin, Ph.D.
WHISKERS ONE

New York • Chicago • San Francisco • Lisbon • London
Madrid • Mexico City • Milan • New Delhi • San Juan
Seoul • Singapore • Sydney • Toronto

The McGraw-Hill Companies

1 2 3 4 5 6 7 8 9 0 DOC/DOC 0 1 0 9 8

ISBN: 978-0-07-160221-1
MHID: 0-07-160221-6

To all my amazing students,
you are also my teachers.

CONTENTS

FOREWORD

With the immaculate timing of a feline, *CATS* appears before you at a unique and appropriate time in the evolution of human intelligence. Since the dawn of civilization, a mere 10,000 years ago, the human race has gone through four significant revolutions and ages and is now entering its fifth.

The first age, which began 10,000 years ago and ended at the start of the eighteenth century, was the agrarian revolution. This saw the settlement of human groups into villages, towns, and cities and the development of agriculture and trade. In the early 1800s, the next great revolution began—one that was to transform the way human beings lived and thought—the industrial revolution. In turn, that led to the industrial age.

In a span of a mere hundred years, to the start of the 1900s, the industrial age had given birth to its own revolution—the information revolution—which then generated the information age, the growth of which was spurred on by radio, television, film, telephone, fax, and the printed media. This is the age in which you were probably born. The information age lasted until very recently—until the 1990s, when it was realized that information was not the be-all and end-all. It was the appropriate organization and structuring of the information that was paramount. This gave rise, at the end of the last millennium, to the short-lived knowledge age, in which information was organized into more manageable chunks and divided into categories.

At the beginning of the twenty-first century, a greater realization occurred, giving rise to an exceptionally exciting new age that might well be the longest—possibly everlasting—age that we humans experience. This was brought about by the realization that far more important than the knowledge of knowledge is the knowledge of the manager of knowledge. And that manager is the super-biocomputer we all possess—our brain. Not only is it necessary to have knowledge of the human brain, but it is also necessary to know how to use it. This knowledge requires a deep understanding of the brain's cognitive functions and the development and application of its multiple intelligences.

The revolution we are now embroiled in at this early part of the twenty-first century is the intelligence revolution. We are taking just the first steps into the intelligence age. One of the first milestones of this era was when Mexico's President Vicente Fox, at the fifth annual United Nations Convention for Creativity and Quality in 2003, declared that this century should be nominated the "century for the development of creativity and innovation."

Shortly after this announcement, *Harvard Business Review* declared, on its October 2004 front cover, that there was a "looming creativity crisis." The British Institute of Management, in a global survey, confirmed that international business leaders felt that the graduates from universities and MBA programs were comparatively "useless" because of their lack of mental flexibility, inability to solve problems, robotic methods of thinking, and demonstrable lack of creativity and inability to innovate. In the last seven years, a number of countries—including China, Singapore, Mexico, Scotland, and Malaysia—have spearheaded initiatives to raise the level of national creativity. Such initiatives were seen as the only way to forge ahead in today's increasingly competitive global marketplace.

In summary, a new globally accepted awareness has emerged. Right now, any individual, company, or country wishing to survive and thrive in the twenty-first century must develop the brain's seemingly infinite capacity to create and innovate. To develop these capacities, you need excellent guidance and your own application to the task. *CATS* will launch you on this journey.

And you will be guided by a master in the field. I have known the lead author of *CATS*, Professor Steve Lundin, for over 20 years. One of the first qualities you look for in a master guide is congruence: Does he or she practice what he or she preaches, and more important, does he or she preach what he or she practices? Steve does. His home and his family flower with creativity. His family is always bubbling with laughter, and laughter is as sure a sign of the presence of creativity as water is to the presence of life. Steve will tell you, in *CATS*, how he uses jogging as his strategic way to give himself a break. He always comes back sweaty and with a new idea. What Steve modestly excludes from this story is that he was an international-level ultra-marathon runner and competitor. Steve gives himself plenty of time to think! He comes back with big ideas! And *CATS* is one of them.

Steve has demonstrated once again that he is a leading master guide to the personal side of innovation. He has conceived a book that is accessible, relevant, and playful and designed to help you apply the excellent lessons you will receive from these pages. Having read and received its wisdom, you most surely will be a more relaxed, active, confident, productive, and innovative person.

You will be, like Steve, a really cool CAT!

TONY BUZAN

Tony Buzan is the originator of Mind Maps®, the thinking tool popularly called the "Swiss army knife" of the brain. He is the world's leading author, lecturer, and advisor to governments, businesses, the professions, universities, and schools on the brain, learning, and thinking skills. In addition, Tony is the founder of the Brain Trust charity and the Use Your Head/Brain Clubs. He is the creator of the concepts Radiant Thinking and Mental Literacy. Tony has written 82 books published in 100 countries and in 30 languages.

BASIC ASSUMPTIONS OF CATS

There were a number of significant assumptions made in the writing of this book.

BASIC ASSUMPTION 1: All human beings have the capacity to innovate. It comes with our membership in the human race.

BASIC ASSUMPTION 2: The Nine Lives are a curriculum for development of our personal innovation capacity. Any one of the Nine Lives, well lived, is a positive step in our personal growth.

BASIC ASSUMPTION 3: We all commit daily acts of innovation. We may not think much about them because they happen naturally.

BASIC ASSUMPTION 4: The human brain is an associative mechanism that constantly builds associative networks. The strong networks are called *routines*, *habits*, and *paradigms*.

BASIC ASSUMPTION 5: Innovation brings vitality, meaning, and novelty into our lives.

BIGGEST BASIC ASSUMPTION 6: Innovative organizations are organizations with a lot of CATS!

A CATS VOCABULARY

In the innovation space, there is a range of meaning for the most common words. We've picked out the words CATS use often and included the definitions used in this book:

- **Idea** A concept or notion that has its origin in the human brain.
- **Novel idea** An original or unusual concept or notion.
- **Creativity** The act of generating a novel idea.
- **Prototype** A mock-up of an idea.
- **Innovation** Fashioning something new and of potential value from a novel idea.
- **Organization** A useful abstraction for a group of people working together. It can, however, keep us from seeing the importance of people when we use the word anthropomorphically.*
- **CAT** and **CATS** are *not* acronyms. The individual letters stand for absolutely nothing.
- **Cat** The common pet that says "meow" and has whiskers.

*I love this word, but I will admit that outside psychology it doesn't get much use. *Anthropomorphic* means to ascribe human characteristics to things that are not human—organizations, for instance. In doing this, we take the focus away from what is real.

- **The CAT inside** The capacity to innovate that comes with membership in the human race.
- **CAT** Anyone working to develop his or her capacity to innovate.
- **CAT Nip** An activity that provokes your thinking or tests your newfound CAT skills.
- **CAT Pause** A break in the action that creates a space for reflection.
- **CAT'S Eye View** A real example of a Life that shows what the Life might look like in action.

ACKNOWLEDGMENTS

I would like to dedicate this book to my students—physically challenged children at Camp Courage, fourth and fifth graders at Webster Elementary School, master's degree students at Texas Tech, MBA and doctoral students at the University of St. Thomas, Metropolitan State University, and the University of Charleston—and members of the audiences who have assembled to hear me talk about *FISH!*®, *Top Performer*®, and *CATS*. You, my students, also have been my teachers, and I celebrate your role in my life with this acknowledgment.

For 20 years, my wife Janell and I managed the Institute for Management Studies (IMS) in Minneapolis–St. Paul. During that time, I attended hundreds of presentations made by some of the best business thinkers in the world. The IMS seminars have been a significant part of my intellectual development. The business provided the resources that allowed us to send our children to college. Thank you Gordon Peters and Cecile Morgan for taking a chance on a young guy at a time when your model was to hire retired executives. I want to acknowledge your personal contribution to my life as well as the contribution made by the organization you created in a moment of insight and innovation. It was a new model for executive education and it has lasted over 30 years.

I also would like to thank the team at Ontend Creative Partners: Carr, Mick, John, Gordy, Amy,

Marian, and Melissa. Your brilliance and creativity are boundless. Carr Hagerman and I founded Ontend Creative Partners, and I couldn't ask for a better business partner and friend. Together we wrote *Top Performer* and produced a film by the same name. He is one of the best-read people I know and is the only person I know who starts his day by reading from the *Oxford English Dictionary*. Together we are building a greenhouse for innovation that will nurture and provide a home for our work in filmmaking, writing, and education. We both use and further develop the ideas in this book on a daily basis.

I thank Jimmy Tan, who contributed to an early version of this manuscript before we went our separate ways. *CATS* is radically different from that early version, but Jimmy helped me get started and for that I am truly grateful.

At age 67, I am somewhat surprised to find myself starting a new chapter in my life at a time when most of my friends are retiring. I must admit that there are times, such as seven hours into a 14-hour transpacific flight, when I think retirement sounds like a good idea, too. What I am doing, however, would make my mentor, John Gardner, founder of Common Cause, author, and statesman, proud. When I interviewed him in the last years of his life, he too was starting a new chapter and was focusing his intellect and writing on the needs of communities. He was 85 and vital. With his example, and God willing, I look forward to my 70s and 80s and wonder, just for a moment, what lies ahead.

I thank my life partner and best friend, my wife Janell. Without Janell at my side for the last 25 years, none of this would have happened. We have lived through the death of a child and the birth of a great-granddaughter. We are grateful for our gifts and for each other, but family will always be first. I love you, Janell.

Finally, I would like to acknowledge not one but two publishers. First, I want to recognize Management Press of the Australian Institute of Management, who published an earlier version of this book in Australia. Thanks to Carolyn Barker, Vivienne Anthon, and Donna Kennedy, who have been great supporters. Carolyn and Vivienne are coauthors of *CATS: The Personal Guide*. Vivienne has provided extensive critiques of the manuscript at each of the various stages and has always been spot on.

I feel like the luckiest guy in the world because I have found an editor who has all the qualities I respect. Herb Schaffner is thoughtful, bright, talented, passionate, hard working, and a great human being. I look forward to our discussions and value his input. Thanks, Herb. I hope we can do this again some day. I want to salute the publisher for whom Herb works, McGraw-Hill, and the staff that have joined with Herb to support this effort. This extraordinary team includes Ed Chupak, Seth Morris, Daina Penikas, Maureen Harper, and Kenya Henderson.

CATS

PART ONE

Innovation Turned Upside Down

It is really quite simple: Innovative organizations are places with innovative people. The strategy question has to be, "How do we develop the capacity to innovate residing in our employees?"

Much of what is written about innovation describes the view from 30,000 feet. My point of view is at sea level. Most of what is written about innovation is geared to the top of the organization. It makes more sense to me to turn the organization upside down. It is my view that employees are the primary source of innovation in an organization.

I believe that all innovation is personal, and to focus exclusively on abstractions such as the organization, strategy, and culture takes our attention away from the true source of all innovation, you and me.

High-altitude articles, books, and white papers often identify a technique or practice found inside a company and suggest that the success of the company is a direct result of that technique or practice. Company X is innovative because it promotes self-managed teams. Company Y is innovative because it hires a diverse workforce. Company Q is not innovative because it has implemented Six Sigma. Company Z is innovative because specific individuals are assigned the role of sponsor. Company J is innovative because the CEO understands discontinuities. Company HR is innovative because it rewards innovation.

Don't misunderstand; the body of high-altitude work is useful and important. As a student of innovation, I read these articles and books with relish. I simply want to make one thing perfectly clear: I believe that we have devoted far too much attention to top executives and an organization's strategy and far too little attention to the primary source of innovation. We have let the CAT out of the bag!

CATS: The Nine Lives of Innovation has a personal focus. I assume that any organization is better off if it has innovative people to populate the strategies, structures, and systems. This is a book about developing the capacity to innovate at all levels of the organization. It is time to turn things upside down.

One recent book, *Innovation to the Core*, comes close to echoing this same view. The authors draw a parallel between the quality movement and the approach to innovation they prescribe. In the quality movement, the early efforts focused on developing specialists in quality. Soon, a massive quality industry emerged that provided quality consulting, quality gurus, quality mouse pads, and quality training. Eventually, it became that an effective quality effort had to involve each member of the organization as a primary source for quality. It became standard practice to view each employee as someone who had a role in quality. In other words, quality was driven to the core of the organization, the individual. Quality was turned upside down.

The case made in *Innovation to the Core* is that innovation, like quality, must be driven to the core and become a responsibility of every employee. For this reason, organizations need to train employees to innovate. I agree.

However, the authors of *Innovation to the Core* stop short of describing what innovation looks like at the personal level and how we should develop the capacity to innovate in individual employees. And that is precisely why I wrote *CATS: The Nine Lives of Innovation*. I wrote it to describe what innovation looks like at the personal level and to provide a curriculum for training individuals in the tools, concepts, and practices of personal innovation. This is a book for any person who wants to develop her* ability to innovate.

---

*I will use *him* or *her* and *she* or *he* randomly so as to avoid the cumbersome combinations or the less grammatical *their*.

CHAPTER 1

All Innovation Is Personal

Fundamentally, We Are the Source of All Innovation

This is a book about innovation. I'll pause while you cover that yawn. Don't be embarrassed, I understand. Okay? Let me start again. This is a book about innovation, but the perspective of the book is personal, and the potential results are both personal and organizational. Is there a little more energy in that?

This is about you, a you that has the potential to be more productive than the present you. This is about a you that can have more vitality at work and greater satisfaction with life. Do I have your full attention now? You see, personal innovation produces the natural energy of life. And natural energy is what gives life its juice. It makes you want to howl.

If you wish to create a vital life, one that is meaningful and deeply satisfying, innovation can help you to get there. Just think about the parts of your life that give you the greatest sense of satisfaction right now. It is often the everyday tasks that provide opportunities for us to innovate. Think about the parts of your life that have energy for you. Aren't they the places where you are engaged in the act of creation? Use the list below to stimulate your memory.

- Organizing a successful fund-raiser for charity
- Mentoring another person and finding ways to help him or her grow
- Finding a faster way to wash the dishes
- Responding to the uniqueness in another
- Doing something routine in a new way
- Trying a new route to work and discovering a new favorite restaurant
- Establishing a family night in a way that engages all ages
- Writing a book, article, or important e-mail in a way that is authentic and original
- Creating a poem, song, or dynamite ditty in the car
- Building a sand castle with your grandchildren
- Building a sand castle without your grandchildren

- Finding a novel way to say "I love you"
- Starting a business
- Starting another business
- Securing a big order
- Having an idea in the shower that solves a problem
- Rearranging the furniture in the family room
- Reinventing your work life
- Building a second revenue stream
- Developing your own form of retirement
- Building on your key values to create your life
- Interacting with a customer in a novel way
- Finding a calm and effective way to get a teenager to clean his or her room
- Finding a compassionate way to get grandpa to stop driving the car

These are all examples of everyday innovation. Not included on the list are momentous discoveries such as finding the cure for ulcers, identifying a new method for locating black holes in space, or earning a Nobel Prize for the development of a new paradigm in economics. These achievements also would have a rightful place on the list, but their inclusion would detract from the key point. Innovation is at the heart of a life well lived. Massive achievement might detract from the main theme, but it in no way would be outside the scope of the Nine Lives. All innovation, big or small, relies on the same basic set of principles, and those principles are all personal. In this book they are organized as the Nine Lives of Innovation.

Life is a great and exciting adventure. It is the little victories that we experience from these everyday innovations that add up to a fulfilling existence. Innovation reminds us that life, authentically lived, is always a precious and amazing journey. Do you have the courage to claim your happiness? You might start by becoming more innovative.

Did Curiosity Really Kill the Cat?

Curiosity is a trait celebrated in cats. Curiosity is also an ingredient in innovation. Cats seem to be attracted to nooks and crannies, but to attribute curiosity exclusively to them is not fair to their human counterparts. Could you imagine innovation without a human being who said, "I wonder what would happen if . . .?"

It is said that curiosity killed the cat. But have you ever seen one die of curiosity? This reminds me of a recent story about a cat that was lodged in the wall of a bar. For two days, men and women worked to release this cat, and ultimately, they were successful. It may have been curiosity that put the cat in this predicament. It may have been hunger or stupidity. One thing is sure: the cat has a real tale to tell his grandchildren when they make their annual trip to the dump. My experience after talking to thousands of potential CATS is that in those few instances when someone thinks he has an example of curiosity killing a cat it turns out to have been a car or a dog, not curiosity.

I believe that old tale about cats and curiosity is designed to keep you in your place, to throttle one of your greatest gifts—your curiosity.

It is also said that a cat has nine lives—a phrase that comes closer to matching my experience with cats. This old saying is the source of the title of this book—*The Nine Lives of Innovation*. It provides structure to a rather diverse set of ingredients that make up innovation.

By accessing the potential of any one of the Nine Lives, we boost our personal ability to innovate. And once we implement any one of the Lives, we can proudly call our self a CAT.

CHAPTER 2

Four Challenges and Nine Lives

The Nine Lives approach to innovation recognizes that there are four basic challenges to innovation and outlines nine ways, called *lives*, to meet these challenges. The focus is on the individual. Personal innovation can occur in everyday things and in major initiatives that are part of a large-scale corporate innovation strategy. The same principles apply to both at the individual level.

The Four Basic Challenges to Innovation

The four challenges represent universal impediments to innovation, and the Nine Lives represent building blocks from which to fashion strategies to overcome the four challenges. Harnessing any one of the lives will move you in the direction of innovation, and the more you harness, the more potent your move will be. Each of the challenges will be immediately recognizable, and each of the lives can be learned. These ideas are neither mutually exclusive nor exhaustive. They are simply my personal assessment of what is most important based on my life experience, which includes my reading of the literature. Another way of saying this is that the Nine Lives of Innovation is my theory as to what is most important to innovation at the fundamental human level.

The four challenges to innovation are not negotiable. They are a part of what it means to be human, so ignoring them is not an option. Each requires a powerful antidote once you have developed a clear understanding of its source of power. The four basic challenges that must be overcome in order to enhance your innovation quotient are:

1. **Distractions.** The doubts and fears accumulated over a lifetime are there, in part, to keep us safe and secure. They are also a major distraction to those who would innovate. They can be a straightjacket preventing innovation. And the "noise" created by the clutter of life can drown out our thoughts and remove all the spaciousness so important to innovation.

2. **Normal.** In order to survive as human beings, we are endowed with the ability to be normal. This means that we develop standard ways to approach life's many challenges, from getting dressed in the morning to avoiding saber-tooth

tigers on the way to work. In different cultures, normal takes different forms. Innovation requires getting outside the norms, and this is no small task given the amount of practice we have simply being normal.

3. **Failure.** Even though failure is fundamental to learning, most of us grow up trying to avoid failure. Who wakes up in the morning saying, "I think I will devote this day to failure"? To make progress, we must come to grips with the importance of failure in learning and innovation. To innovate, we must understand and at times even embrace failure.

4. **Leadership.** Creativity is a quality that can't be directed, coerced, or controlled as if it were an assigned location in the corporate parking lot. Typical leadership techniques often create an environment that is conducive to some things but toxic for innovation. The challenge to leadership is to collaborate in the provision of a climate full of "natural energy." I call those who accept this challenge *CAT Wranglers*.

The Nine Lives of Innovation

The challenges listed above are both real and ubiquitous. My principle-based solutions are an antidote to the toxic nature of the challenges and provide fundamental steps in the personal innovation journey. They are called the *Nine Lives of Innovation* because each of the lives will move you in the direction of greater personal innovation. In other words, these remedies can help innovation come alive in a world naturally full of challenges.

The impact of these lives well lived will be seen in increased personal innovation, and because human beings populate organizations, their organizations will be described as more innovative and having a higher quality of work life. Let's go through the Nine Lives:

1. **CATS create an innovation friendly environment.** There is a constant conversation going on in most minds that must be quieted in order to provide the spaciousness needed for innovation. Clutter also takes the form of distractions of this crazy world that seems to generate new distractions daily.

2. **CATS are always prepared.** Innovation favors a prepared mind. The way you organize your experience in the warehouses we call *memory* can serve you well when it comes time to innovate.

3. **CATS know that innovation isn't normal.** One way to counter the effects of being normal is to understand how and why we humans have evolved the way we have. If we didn't have a routine for most things we do, life would be a long linear sequence of choices. However, while the routine allows us to be human beings, it also can inhibit our ability to innovate. We need to understand this paradox to understand the role of provocation.

4. **CATS welcome physical provocation.** To escape from the clutches of what is normal, we can provoke ourselves with objects and other physical provocations.

5. **CATS enjoy social provocation.** A conversation can be provocative if we allow ourselves to use the ideas of others for their movement value as well as their content. There is nothing quite so electric as a group of CATS in conversation. The fur really flies.

6. **CATS promote intellectual provocation.** To escape the containing power of the norm, we can stimulate our thinking with positive mental assaults and imaginary provocations.

7. **CATS say "How fascinating!"** A great way to meet failure is with whimsy. "My goodness, I invested in this startup, and it didn't survive." After the initial whammy and shock, innovators, like entrepreneurs, have the capacity to say, "How fascinating! What can I learn from this?"

8. **CATS fail early and fail well.** Since failure is always a part of the formula for innovation, and since a certain amount of failure is needed in order to learn important lessons along the way, one thing becomes clear: CATS learn how to get failure out of the way early so the maximum amount of learning can occur. This approach facilitates innovation and minimizes the cost of failure.

9. **CAT Wranglers understand natural energy.** Leadership plays a significant role in the overall innovation process of any organization. Our focus is on the role of leadership in nurturing, developing, and supporting individuals in a way that ensures the energy is natural. CAT Wranglers provide a safe environment for CATS to play.

Please note that I am not tackling the whole process of innovation, but only the development of people, CATS, who will be ready, willing, and able to innovate—whatever the process.

Earning a CAT Belt

In Chapter 6 of this book I provide tools for those CATS who wish to sustain what they have learned in the book as they continue to prowl through life. Some CATS may even be interested in teaching a whole new litter. The CAT Belts are meant to be a fun way to accomplish both.

CAT Nip

Can you think of an innovation moment you have experienced recently?

CHAPTER 3

The Four Challenges to Innovation

A deep understanding of the four challenges is important to a CAT. We are all somewhat familiar with most or all of these challenges; we experience most of them on a daily basis. A CAT must understand the four challenges inside out in order to truly appreciate the need for the Nine Lives.

The First Challenge: Doubts, Fears, and Distractions

The world is full of clutter, noise, and distraction. Car horns, loud music, comments made by detractors, the voice of a former teacher, the voice of judgment in our head, and countless other sources of clutter affect us. On top of all this is our own personal collection of doubts and fears.

Innovation makes some of us quite nervous because it implies change. One way to keep things the same and avoid the change of innovation is to plant the seeds of fear. And, as noted in Chapter 1, this may be the origin of the statement, "Curiosity killed the cat"—to create fear in others so that they don't stir things up with all sorts of ideas that mess up the status quo. I believe that sayings like this one are born out of fear, not real experience. But they are nevertheless a challenge.

But let's take another spin on curiosity. It is a natural human trait that fuels our growth from the time we are born. Philosopher Tom Morris has gone so far as to suggest that creativity is the meaning of life itself. The quality of our life depends on the release of our own unique brand of creativity. And this internal drive is powerful. Who can be creative without being curious?

We are also bombarded with the clutter of life. The noise created by the clutter of life can drown out thoughts and remove all the spaciousness so important to innovation. In other words, the clutter and distractions keep our minds occupied, often with trivia, leaving no opportunity to innovate.

Being busy has become a badge of honor for some. It is as if being really busy means we've somehow "made it." Yet we haven't made it until we also realize what busyness and clutter take from us, as well as what they possibly may give us. Maybe this is why there are always books on the best-seller list that promote the beauty of simplicity, the joy of spaciousness, and the power of being in the now.

The following recent experience will provide a quick example of the clutter and distractions that have penetrated every part of our lives. I was on the road and having a meal alone at a restaurant. When I am alone, I like to observe people, so I was tuned to the people around me and what they were doing. At one table, a family of four was having a night out together. There was mom and dad and kids, who were probably 12 and 8. The thing that was amazing to me was they were all on their mobile phones. They were all talking to someone not present at the table. This brings a new and rather sad meaning to "family night out." I have observed similar behavior in all corners of this world. We carry devices with us that have the capacity to keep us from having the space to innovate.

This is what I mean by distractions and clutter. It is not just the car horns and train whistles, but a host of things we carry around with us to be sure we have no peace of mind.

Find a place of solitude, and just listen to the voices inside your head.

After listening to the voices on the inside, turn your attention to the noise on the outside.

Just listen.

CAT Nip

Think of a time when you were devastated by the comments of a thoughtless critic.

- What was your idea?
- What did the voice of judgment say?
- How did that feel?
- What did you think but not say out loud?
- What did you say? What did you do then?
- Did you fight back or give up?
- What are the long-term effects of this drama if it is played over and over again?
- How can you stop the drama from playing in your life?

Now find someone to talk about this with, and see what his experience has been with critics.

The Second Challenge: Being Normal

Our evolution as humans has provided a powerful survival tool. We can develop habits, routines, and protocols that allow us to function and protect us from harm. This is a good thing, with only a few exceptions. Innovation is one exception.

Fortunately and Unfortunately, All CATS Are Normal

It is quite natural for cats to spend time in or around boxes. Loving owners of cats provide

Tabby with that well-known convenience, the "cat box." A cardboard box on the floor will always attract a cat, who can play for hours—leaping about, hiding, pouncing, stalking, and, you know, just being a cat. For humans, it is another type of box that is of greater concern: the construct of routine—a critical life tool on the one hand and a cage that prevents innovative exploration on the other. Let's call this a CAT Box as well. This type of CAT Box represents a vital human capacity without which we might not survive as a species, but it is also a potential barrier to innovation. Now this is a dilemma!

The CAT Box may be described as "normal," or you may have heard it described as a "routine" or "paradigm." The term has taken on such popular use that in fact you may simply hear it referred to as "the box." This box keeps CATS from innovating because it is so hard to escape from established routines. Old ways of doing things are actually hard-wired in the brain; they have a physical manifestation. From a daily life perspective, "routines" are crucial to making our way in a complex world. Consider getting dressed or driving a car if there were no routine, and each and every step along the way had to be considered in the light of all possibilities in order to decide what to do next. We could spend our whole life doing nothing but getting dressed or backing the car out of the garage.

Why does a car have reverse gear? This may seem like an odd question, but let's approach it scientifically. Suppose that you were doing a simple cost-benefit analysis and found that your car is in reverse gear for 0.001 percent of the time, but to have reverse gear costs about $500. It would seem to be a lot of money for such a small amount of use. But reverse gear is to a car as creativity is to normal. When you need it, you need it badly. Being normal is just fine for much of your life, but when you need a new idea, it requires escaping from the bonds of normal.

There is no better illustration of the phenomenon of being chained to "normal" than that of the elephants of Thailand. In rural Thailand, where elephants are an integral part of life, when calves are young, they are shackled by the leg to a wooden post. The young elephants eventually give up all resistance. Being chained to a post has become "normal."

Older elephants could easily rip the post out of the ground, but they don't. They have become accustomed to the routine. The following are some other examples of normal in action. Notice that each and every one of the individuals mentioned is extremely bright and highly productive. Normal is, well, you know, normal.

"640K ought to be enough for anybody"—Bill Gates, founder of Microsoft, 1981.

"I think there is a world market for maybe five computers"—Thomas Watson, Jr., chairman of IBM, 1943.

"Heavier-than-air flying machines are impossible"—Lord Kelvin, president of the Royal Society in Great Britain, 1895.

"There is no need for any individual to have a computer in his home"—KEN OLSON, PRESIDENT OF DIGITAL EQUIPMENT, 1977.

"No matter what he does, he will never amount to anything"—ALBERT EINSTEIN'S TEACHER, 1895.

"I have traveled the length and breadth of this country and talked with the best people, and I can assure you that data processing is a fad that won't last out this year"—THE EDITOR IN CHARGE OF BUSINESS BOOKS FOR PRENTICE-HALL, 1957.

"This telephone has too many shortcomings to be seriously considered as a means of communication. This device is inherently of no value to us"—WESTERN UNION INTERNAL MEMO, 1876.

"Who the hell wants to hear actors talk?"—H. M. WARNER, WARNER BROTHERS, 1927.

"Everything that can be invented has been invented"—CHARLES H DUELL, COMMISSIONER OF THE U.S. OFFICE OF PATENTS, 1899.

"We don't like their sound, and guitar music is on the way out"—DECCA RECORDING COMPANY, REJECTING THE BEATLES, 1962.

"Airplanes are interesting toys but of no military value"—MARECHAL FERDINAND FOCH, PROFESSOR OF STRATEGY, ECOLE SUPERIEURE DE GUERRE, 1911.

"Drill for oil? You mean drill in the ground to try to find oil? You're crazy"—DRILLERS APPROACHED BY EDWIN L. DRAKE, 1859.

"Stocks have reached what looks like a permanently high plateau"—IRVING FISHER, PROFESSOR OF ECONOMICS, YALE UNIVERSITY, 1929.

"Louis Pasteur's theory of germs is ridiculous fiction"—PIERRE PACHET, PROFESSOR OF PHYSIOLOGY AT TOULOUSE, 1872.

"We're selling about five pacemakers a month now; I think we've saturated the market"—EARL BAKKEN, FOUNDER OF MEDRONIC AND INVENTOR OF THE BATTERY-OPERATED PACEMAKER.

Note that these are accomplished people who completely underestimated the possibilities. CATS in organizations often become so acclimatized to the systems and routines that they fail to see the possibilities that a 10-degree turn of their head would reveal. They are capable of pulling the post out of the ground but are numbed by what has been accepted as the norm.

The following exercises provide a few simple activities that will help you to get a quick idea of the power and importance of normal. It is a beginning on the path to understanding our own paradigms. Notice how awkward it is to do something common in a different way.

Associative Boundaries

Associative boundaries provide another perspective on the challenge of being normal. We humans have a tendency to exert our dominion over complex things by organizing them. We organize knowledge into disciplines, our lives into roles, and our organizations into departments. In general, these structures help us to operate efficiently and effectively in the world. But disciplines have a tendency to become isolated, departments become silos, and roles become fixed. We say, "This is the role of marketing, and that is the role of sales. This is engineering, and that is medicine. This is who I am, and that is not." What was created to serve us can become a limiting factor for personal innovation. This is so because much of innovation occurs at the intersection of the boundaries between disciplines, departments, and roles.

Frans Johansson, in his book, *The Medici Effect*, describes dozens of examples of innovation at the intersection. He also highlights the importance of associative boundaries as a challenge to innovation. The stronger a person's associative boundaries, the harder it is for that person to see the innovative connections between things that are not in the same category. Our ability to "see" the innovative ideas at the edge requires that we weaken our associative boundaries. This is one challenge of being normal. We all have these boundaries.

Think about your associative boundaries. What parts of your life are so well developed they may have solidified?

Think about your professional boundaries, such as banker, accountant, customer service agent, manager, biologist, surgeon, or sales associate.

Consider your departmental boundaries, such as what should properly take place in research, human resources, administration, sales, marketing, quality, accounting, and operations.

Consider your cultural boundaries.

Do you have childrearing boundaries, strongly held beliefs about the right way to raise children?

Do you have gender boundaries, what one gender should do or not do?

Consider your boundaries for a moment. How flexible are your boundaries?

CAT Nip

Feel the Power of Normal

- Cross your arms. Now cross them the other way. Why was that so uncomfortable?
- Extend the left hand for a handshake.
- Take a different route to work.
- Sit in a different pew at church.
- If you usually go out the back door, start going out the front door.
- Park your car in a different spot in long-term airport parking. (But make good notes if you are a frequent flyer.)
- End your evening meal with a prayer.
- Try a different sequence in the morning.
- Brush your teeth with the other hand.

- Wear your watch on the other wrist.

Ask someone close to you to describe your most obvious routines. Change one of them for a couple days. How did that feel? How long do you think it would take to make a new routine feel comfortable?

As you have seen from this discussion and the Nips and Pauses presented, much of our life is lived in routine ways. With our routines, we can navigate through life safely and without a lot of thought. This is a good thing unless we are crossing the street in London (and you are from a country that drives on the right side of the road). Then it can be downright dangerous. Unfortunately, these life-affirming routines get in the way when your want to innovate. (Not quite as dangerous as crossing the street in London, but with their own set of challenges.)

What is harder to see is that our intellectual life also has its routines. We have routine ways of thinking about things, approaching problems, and organizing experiences. Our reliance on these normal ways of thinking about things also can be a barrier to innovation. And trying new ways of thinking is just as awkward as changing physical routines. But breaking routines is our route to the novel. Being normal is a challenge.

Consider the following statements that represent a way of thinking we all encounter at some point in our life:

- "That's the way we've always done it here."
- "If it ain't broke, don't fix it."

Can you add a couple of your own?

The Third Challenge: Failure

When we are infants, we are willing to try anything and often do. As we get older, we continue to explore the world, but we begin to get adult feedback about what is and isn't okay. We love to explore and try different things and will often use colors in ways adults don't consider normal. They worry about us making fools of ourselves in school and being criticized for being outside what is considered normal. Then it happens. We make a mistake, and someone laughs at us in a way we know is not complementary. It stings. When it happens a second time, we decide we don't like it. We seek to avoid this unpleasant feeling in the future. We make sure that our possibility of failing is limited. We take fewer risks. This is the beginning of our journey on the road to fearing failure.

There is an often-used exercise that highlights the development of our fear of failure. People are organized in pairs and asked to have a piece of paper and a pencil available. Without warning or preparation, they are then asked to begin drawing a sketch of the other person's face. After an uncomfortable minute or two, they are asked to stop and show the other person what they have drawn. Most participants spend the time apologizing for not being able to do a better job. There is a great deal of angst.

The group then discusses what this activity would have been like if they were five or six years old. All agree that it would have been fun and pleasurable to do the same task at five. The discussion then turns to the difference. The thing that has changed is years of judgement by others and our desire not to hurt someone's feelings. Think about this. What is good, and what is unfortunate?

Fear of Failure

In the work world, fear of failure is common. Great effort is taken to avoid mistakes and eliminate flubs, flops, glitches, guffaws, stumbles, fumbles, snags, screw-ups, dropped balls, mess-ups, and nicks. This alternative language is testimony to our desire to avoid even saying the word *failure*. It loses sight of the fact that failure is the foundation of learning and that innovation depends on a healthy diet of failure, especially when you work in a low-tolerance organization. To eliminate failure would mean eliminating learning and innovation. But the fear is real.

A clever way to show how silly this is comes from a Tony Buzan presentation, and I paraphrase it here: A baby is internally driven to push the limits. While learning to stand and walk, the baby falls hundreds of times. But have you ever seen a baby give up and say, "Oh, the hell with it. I'll stay on the floor for the rest of my life." Babies don't know about failure yet; they are simply driven to learn to walk.

The Challenge of Failing Poorly

When fear of failure dominates, it is hard to think of failing well. We know about failing well early in life. We don't learn how to ride a bike by starting on a steep hill covered with rocks. We start with training wheels and with dad or mom running behind. We try to minimize the bleeding by failing well. When we settle into a job, however, we often fail poorly by covering up what needs to be brought to the surface and discussed and by trying to think everything through before starting. There is also the nasty habit of running with a project and working hard only to find that we have done the wrong project. It doesn't matter how carefully and professionally we do a project if it is the wrong project. These are some of the challenges of failure.

CAT Nip

See if you can summarize your approach to failure and communicate it to a friend.

Think for a moment about your most spectacular failures and what you learned from them.

The Fourth Challenge: Leadership and Energy

The final barrier to innovation is a leadership barrier. When innovation occurs within an organization, a special breed of leadership is required—a brand of leader who is focused on releasing energy rather than consuming it.

It is important to remember that not everyone welcomes innovation. Innovation, by definition, means change, and as we have discussed, we humans are wired for routine. Yet, while our short-term survival requires routine, our long-term survival has required significant change. So we are, in fact, capable of significant change. And leadership can help or get in the way.

In an organization, we often bring our personal skills to teams, and members of our teams will vary in terms of their willingness to innovate. This is where leadership can make a major contribution.

While the volume of material available on leadership is immense, that which is addressing the relationship of leadership to innovation at a personal level is much smaller. And within that set of things that apply to the leadership needed to support personal innovation, one aspect is dominant: Innovation thrives in an environment filled with natural energy and dies in an environment full of toxic energy. The challenge for leaders is how to eliminate the toxic and attract the natural.

CATS tend to have a serious independent streak, and sometimes they don't play well with others. This also makes it important to have CAT Wranglers in the mix. Their job is to create a CAT-friendly environment.

CATS are also sensitive, and innovating makes them feel vulnerable. This vulnerability requires the delicate leadership of and the special skills of CAT Wranglers. CAT Wranglers respect freedom, eliminate barriers, support divergence, protect vulnerable ideas, and put their own egos aside in favor of serving CATS. Unfortunately, these qualities are different from the qualities we typically find in practice. We don't breed many CAT Wranglers, and that is a big challenge to innovation.

Think of a time when you and those around you didn't feel comfortable adding your unique and personal contributions at work. What was the nature of the leadership?

CAT Nip

Discuss the following topics with a friend:

- Toxic work environments I have experienced or witnessed.
- Moments when I lose energy at work.

Okay. Enough with the negative! It is time to find the positive response to the four challenges. This would be the Nine Lives.

CHAPTER 4

The Nine Lives of Innovation

The *Nine Lives of Innovation* are the heart and soul of this book. All that we have covered to this point has been preparation for the Nine Lives. With one exception, you can start anywhere in the Nine Lives. Each of these lives is independent and will move you to a higher level of innovation capability. They each take you a step closer to being a fully contributing CAT within your organization and in your life.

The one exception is that Life 3: Understanding Normal should precede the three provocation sections, Life 4: Physical Provocation, Life 5: Social Provocation, and Life 6: Intellectual Provocation. This is so because, without a full understanding of normal, the provocations are without clear foundation and can be dismissed. With an understanding of normal, it is clear that provocation is the only reasonable path to innovation.

You will find the Nine Lives accessible and easy to put to use. If your history with innovation has been less than stellar, or if you have always felt that you were genetically programmed not to be innovative, please give the lives a chance. The lives will show you that the opposite is true. Your are *ready*, and if you are *willing*, you soon will be *able*.

Beware that you might just find yourself pouncing on ideas in a way that surprises you. This will prove to you that the CAT has always been inside, waiting for the opportunity you are now providing.

Good luck on your journey, and if you want to maximize your benefits, invite a friend to join you, or better yet, form a CATS' tour group. Nothing is quite as much fun as a herd of CATS on a journey together.

Remember to stay alert as you work through the Nine Lives. You may just encounter a personal *innovation moment*. If you do, pause and write it down.

LIFE 1

CATS Create an Innovation Friendly Environment

The modern world is full of noise. The innovator occasionally must find a place of silence and at times a sense of playfulness to access her full potential.

Whether a cacophony of caterwauls or a simple catfight, life is full of noise. And in the middle of all that noise, sometimes compounding the distraction of the din, there are voices of judgment coming from the past, present, and future. These unwanted voices are criticizing and evaluating every single thing we try to make happen in the world. This is why a CAT must find ways to quiet the mind and open a space for innovation by moving the clutter of life into the background or by finding ways to use the clutter as a provocation.

Of course, there is the rare CAT who relishes the clutter and finds it soothing. He looks at the piles of papers on his desk, floor, and any flat surface and says, "I know where everything is!" For these CATS, clutter is comfortable, and neatness would be distracting. This is what is fun about CATS. They come in all shapes and sizes. And just when you think you have one all figured out, she disappears under a couch.

Is Innovation about Releasing or Learning?

There are experts who believe that all you have to do to have innovation is find a way to remove the effects of your nasty first grade teacher who hated your vulnerable little drawing of a flower. Once the latent effects of that evil person are removed or overcome, you will be free to create, and the ideas will flow.

Another point of view is that your ability to innovate is based on tools and concepts that can be taught, and once you have learned them, your ability to innovate will grow. My belief and my experience are that both are true. This life is focused on freeing you to innovate. The rest of the lives are about the tools, techniques, and concepts. Consider the following vignette as a way to think about the distinction.

A man has been bound with ropes, blindfolded, and tossed into a deep pit. The man struggles and eventually releases his bonds and takes off his blindfold. He leaps to his feet and shouts, "I'm free." True, in a sense, but he is still in a pit. The ropes are the things that keep you from offering what you have to the pursuit of innovation. The wall of the pit represents all those things that are yet to be learned so that you can have more to offer. Both are important.

Voices of Judgment

There is a powerful challenge to all CATS. The conscious and unconscious thoughts of a CAT are frequently full of doubts and fears. Often, just as a

CAT is beginning a creative effort, a voice says, "You're not good enough." "It will never work." "Remember what a fool you made of yourself the last time you tried something like this?" These voices can be the actual voices of those around you, or they can be internal voices that only you can hear. To innovate, a CAT must either silence the voices or weaken their ability to keep her from taking the actions she needs to make her contributions to the world.

The most difficult external voices are the ones closest to home. These are often voices of loved ones and friends who think they are doing what is best for us by keeping us from doing something that has a high risk of failing.

You know, like innovation, for instance.

The Criticism of Family and Friends

In your mind's eye is a beautiful painting with all the vivid details. In your mind's eye is a storyline that you *know* is good. In your mind's eye you see how a number of different forces might interact to create a unique opportunity. In your mind's eye is a product or service sure to make the world a better place. It is only natural that you want to share your insights with those closest to you. Beware. Sharing is not always a good idea!

When you describe what you "see," some of the clarity is lost owing to the limitations of time and language. In fact, when you first express an idea, it may sound a bit lame. When those close to you, some of whom aren't comfortable with you as a creative being anyway, hear you present this partially formed idea, the reaction is often quick. They caution, criticize, and question what you are doing.

At first, it doesn't make sense that the loudest external voices of judgment and the strongest critics are often friends, family, and colleagues. But friends and family like us the way we are and don't really want us to change. Family worries that we might fail or waste our time. They don't want us to get hurt. Colleagues can be threatened that we might succeed and the implications that success would have for them.

So don't expect immediate backing from those you might think will be most supportive. If you feel the need for emotional support, find other innovators to hang with. If not, just do your thing in silence until you have some momentum. Once your direction is clear and you speak with confidence, friends and family will all be on your side again. It's the infancy and transition phase that is most difficult to survive.

So it is usually wise to keep an idea to yourself for a while and give it room to breathe. A new idea is vulnerable and needs to be kept under wraps until it gains some strength and clarity.

The Stakes Are High

If you don't find a way to release yourself from whatever bonds that keep you from being creative, such as the inner voice of judgment, you will never be able to maximize your potential. To find a way out of the pit, you first must be able to remove the prejudices that blind you and free yourself from the inhibitions that bind you. Quieting the voices or overcoming the clutter is an ongoing and important part of a creative life.

Innovative people have multiple ways to silence or at least weaken the voices of judgment. Writers talk about their angel. The composer drowns out the voice of judgment when his head fills with the sound of the music he is creating. The business person grounds herself in core values to find the right path.

The voices of judgment will appear anytime we are engaged in the creative process. We need to consider our strategy to deal with these voices. For example:

- You may hear voices, but you don't have to keep listening.
- You may hear voices, but you don't have to engage in conversation.
- You may hear voices and, in fact, use them as material from which to build success.
- You can use the voices, say hello, and move on.
- You can see the voices as a sign that you are getting close to something important.
- You can use the voices to help you focus.
- You can use the voices like an alarm clock to wake you up.

CAT Nip

Try something that has the potential to instantly create spaciousness in your life. When you find yourself evaluating or judging, redirect your attention to curiosity and wonder. Try to see the same thing with the open interest of an infant. The world looks different when you simply see it and don't judge it.

Busyness

The voices of judgment can snuff out creative juices. Another source of noise that can stifle innovative potential is the anxieties and busyness that clutter your life. How long can you go without checking your personal digital assistant? How often do phone calls interrupt you during the day? How many unnecessary meetings did you attend this week? How many e-mails do you receive each day? How many people with whom you work use the "Reply all" choice when sending an e-mail? Your answers to these and similar questions will start to identify the amount of clutter in your life. With the number of distractions in our lives, it is a wonder that we get anything done.

Many innovators who have been asked where they first had the novel idea that led to their innovation have identified the shower or the car. These places historically have been places of relative calm where the mind is free of intense thought. When you let a phone violate the calm of a car, though, its potential as a place of innovation is lost.

Find ways to free yourself from the clutter that chokes your world. Begin to experience the spaciousness that allows your imagination to take flight. Identify pockets of serenity in empty rooms and out-of-the-way places and states of mind, and bring them into your life.

Building a Greenhouse for Innovation

When Tom Kelley of IDEO said space is the new frontier, he was not talking about the solar system or the galaxy. He was talking about a frontier for innovation. He believes that the arrangement of people at work and the "feel" of the work environment can be managed to serve innovation.

Not surprisingly, IDEO is one of the world's most innovative organizations. This organization has won more awards for design than its competition and has helped over 3,000 businesses create new products or services. I will return to this amazing firm a number of times because it has captured my imagination and respect. There is much to learn about innovation simply observing IDEO. One thing IDEO understands is the importance of workspace to innovation.

To visit an IDEO office is a treat for the senses. Things have changed over the years, but when I first visited the IDEO offices, there were bicycles hanging from the ceiling, one of the teams met under the wing of a DC3, team space was organized in open clusters, and a soft-tip dart often would fly by. The space and the employees were playful. It was a greenhouse for innovation. IDEO

General Manager Tom Kelley was my guide through the greenhouse. It did not escape my attention that Tom believed space was the last frontier of innovation, yet to be fully exploited. And IDEO was a living example of the exciting ways space could become a greenhouse for ideas.

Other Greenhouse Examples

Over the years, I have seen real-life examples and read stories about workspace design and its relationship to an organization's goals. A Scandinavian company messed with its space by painting clouds on the ceilings. Another company removed all names and numbers from the office doors so that you would have to ask for help. In asking for help, you had a chance to have a conversation, and the company wanted to facilitate cross-boundary conversations.

At Imation, a 3M spin-off that has pixie dust in its logo, a windowed bridge between two buildings became a colorful and creative communication center. Markers were placed on the window sills, and those passing would use them to write something on the glass. Everything from graffiti to great new ideas appeared. The window makes a strong statement about the culture.

A Personal Greenhouse You Can Carry with You

The work of Tony Buzan includes an innovation called a Mind Map®. It has a radiant design and is full of color and images. Instead of listing things in a linear fashion, the branches of a Mind Map radiate from the center and branch outward. People who use Mind Map carry varicolored pens and unlined paper with them. When I sit at a conference table with my colored pens in front of me, it is often a source of considerable interest and sometimes skepticism. This can change by the end of the meeting. The radiant design with its key branches representing key topics allows me to follow a moving conversation and to cluster items together, even though they are separate in time. It is not uncommon for others to ask for copies and to review my notes. And it is all on one colorful page!

For me, mind mapping is effective and playful. It is hard to Mind Map without noticing a lightness settling onto your spirit. So I think of mind mapping as a portable way to keep my personal space playful. There are a number of other reasons I map like this, including getting everything on one page and seeing connections. For the purposes of this first life of innovation, however, playfulness is enough. In the second life, the Mind Map can be an important tool for preparation.

Work made fun gets done and done more creatively.

Writing the book *FISH!* was the entry point to a decade of intense learning for me. As I spoke to people about the principles of FISH!®, I found a deep desire across the globe to have a bit more fun at work. One of the four principles of FISH! was play. It was play that was usually first to attract a person's attention, like forbidden fruit, and it was play that was most resisted.

Apparently, someone had spread a rumor that play had no place at work. They might as well have said that innovation has no place at work, knowing what we know about the connection of playfulness to innovation.

So I have devoted 10 years of my life to speaking about the virtues of a light heart and the importance of play in the creation of a nontoxic work climate. I have heard about or seen hundreds, perhaps thousands, of innovations born out of this connection. For example:

- A global call center created a more playful culture and improved retention by 50 percent.
- A large nursing home chain created a work environment where employees not only looked after the physical needs of the residents but also nourished their soul and spirit.
- An automobile dealership went from the bottom to the top of customer service and staff satisfaction measures while improving profits dramatically.
- A private hotel located in the wrong part of town with long established competitors developed a reputation as a fun place to go and became first in class.
- The neural ward of a hospital, usually a difficult place to staff because of the intense needs of the patients, developed a waiting list because word got out that it was a fun place to work.

- The staff of a crisis center for women reduced staff burnout by finding ways to add a little levity to the time not spent with clients.
- A receptionist put a sign on her desk reading, "Manager of Incoming Attitudes."
- A manufacturing floor covered the walls with artwork painted by the children of the workers, and the atmosphere became fully human.

Ponder this: The most innovative organizations are also playful places. They are not stiff and formal. There is no rule that says because you are a professional, you have to act like a stiff.

The Stillness Created by a Powerful Vision

A powerful vision will pull us through the times of doubt and allow us to focus on what has to happen next. We can formulate a vision that is so compelling that it overwhelms our fears. We may hear the voices of judgment, but we can choose to turn a deaf ear and fix on the vision as a north star to guide us.

Vision has served men and women well throughout the ages. Pyramids, paper clips, and pacemakers all began as a raw and imperfect vision. Next time you are traveling along one of the many freeways that ring the major cities of the world or are riding in a cab through the business section of a metropolitan area, look out of the window and read the names on the buildings.

In New York, you would see UPS and 3M; in Singapore, you would see Sony and Singapore Airlines; in London, you would see Cadbury and Burberry; and in Sydney, you would see Qantas and the Commonwealth Bank. Behind those logos there are years of innovation and hard work, and in every case, at the beginning of each and every innovation, there was a human being with a vision.

Every organization began with a vision, but these visions were not always fully developed. Sometimes the vision was just a glimmer on the edge of consciousness. 3M began to take the form we see today when someone had the wild idea that if you attached a little sand on a piece of paper it might be useful as an abrasive. Today, 3M has tens of thousands of products in a variety of industries.

I used to drive around the Twin Cities of Minneapolis and St. Paul and look at the major corporate headquarters located there. As I passed a large building sporting a well-known logo, I would think to myself, "That company started as an idea." It is important to remember that these organizations, from Cargill to the Leukemia Society, were not planted in that location fully grown. Each began as an idea in the mind's eye of an entrepreneur.

CAT Nip

- Can you think of some personal examples of workplaces that seem, by their very nature, to breed fun and innovation?

- Ask yourself this question: "When do I have the most fun at work?"
- Now ask yourself: "When am I most innovative at work?"

A farmer had an old dog. One day his old dog fell into a dry well. At first, the farmer was at a loss as to what to do. I suppose the dog also was at a loss. Then the farmer said to himself, "It's an old dog. Why don't I put an end to its misery. He could either starve to death, or I can bury the dog and cover up the well at the same time?" (As a dog owner, I hate this part, but it is a good story for making a point.)

So the farmer started shoveling the dirt into the well. At first, the dog barked furiously, and the farmer felt sad but had no real choice. Then there was absolute silence. Guessing that the dog was now under the dirt, the farmer looked down. The dog was wagging his tail and looking up at the farmer. He realized that each time he pushed the dirt into the well, the dog would just shake it off and get on top of the pile. The old dog eventually "rode" the pile of new dirt to the top.

Do you allow yourself to be buried under the clutter of life, or do you shake off all the dirt, get on top of the situation, and reframe the dirt as part of your experience base?

A CAT'S Eye View of Life 1

Creating Spaciousness

An author finishes a manuscript on innovation and takes a Father's Day nap. During the nap, his subconscious has an idea that it presents forcefully. The idea: Finish each life with a description of what that life might look like in action. He wakes and writes the idea down on a notebook reserved for such situations. He decides to ask his publisher for a short extension in order to incorporate the idea in the book—from a CAT'S point of view, of course.

Silencing the Voices

An architect finds that her critic shows up to judge her work whenever she considers an idea that is outside her normal routine. She decides to create an imaginary angel who gently silences the critic by singing her favorite song. She smiles, says goodbye to the critic, and continues.

LIFE 2

CATS Are Prepared for Innovation

You can be ready for innovation even though you don't know when an opportunity will present itself. Innovation favors a prepared mind.

An innovation journey requires a certain amount of preparation. CATS prepare when they want to innovate. If you want to innovate in biology, it helps to know a little bit about biology. If you want to innovate in chemistry, it helps to know the periodic table. Being a CAT is not a passive thing. CATS are always learning and growing. A CAT keeps the bags packed. He knows that the opportunity to innovate can appear without warning.

How do you prepare for something if you don't really know what it is or when or if it will happen? How do you prepare for the important but unforeseen? Innovation is like that. You are never quite sure when the need or opportunity to innovate will occur, but this doesn't mean that you can't prepare. In fact, innovation favors a prepared mind.

Was It Luck, and What Is Preparation?

There is a story about a golfer playing the last hole of the British Open on a course where some of the green-side bunkers were so deep that a golfer in the trap actually would be hidden from view. The golfer was in such a bunker, and the championship was on the line. He was tied for the lead. His ball was, in fact, resting just a few inches from a wall of wooden supports holding back the earth in this gargantuan bunker. The sand was coarse, and his ball was partially buried. He took a full swing with an open-faced sand wedge, the ball shot straight up, cleared the top of the bunker, arched ever so slightly toward the green, bounced once on the fringe and twice on the green, and rolled into the cup. By the time the golfer scrambled up to where he could see the green, it was over, but he certainly knew what had happened because the gallery had erupted in applause.

He tipped his hat and walked over to the pin, pretending not to believe the ball was actually in the hole as he peeked between fingers held to his eyes. He smiled and the crowd laughed with him as he hesitantly reached down and retrieved the ball, the flagstick still in place. He gave the crowd a final bow to continued applause. As he left the green, one spectator shouted, "You have to admit that was a lucky shot!" Our hero turned to face the man. He seemed pensive for a brief moment and then responded with a smile, "Lucky it was, without a doubt, but I have noticed over my career as a golfer that the more I practice a shot, the luckier I get."

Random Access to Knowledge

We live in a time when powerful search engines allow us to scan a near-infinite number of digital storage bins for information. It has been my experience, and the experience of many working creatives with whom I've discussed this subject, that the most important information for innovation is that which is immediately available—the kind of information that is stored in a quick-retrieval format in the brain. The reason for this is quite simple: Innovation "feeds off" a quick response to provocation. Only what you carry with you and can access quickly is available in the moment you are provoked.

This makes it important to consider what you carry with you and how you store it. How do you store your knowledge? Do you just let it accumulate, or do you attempt to organize it for maximum benefit? If you find a way to organize your brain, then when an innovation moment comes up, you will be prepared.

What Do You Carry with You?

When we pack our bags for a long trip, we usually know ahead of time whether we are going to the seashore or the mountains. With innovation, it is often different. We don't know for sure where we will end up, nor do we fully understand the route that will take us there. So the more contingencies for which we can prepare, the better.

While the bags we pack for a trip are cumbersome and the storage limited, the storage space for the bags we take to the land of innovation is virtually infinite. When it comes to innovation, we can put all the possessions we will need in a small, fist-sized compartment called the *brain*. But just like packing our physical bags, the time and attention we spend in storage are also rewarded.

How would you describe the universe of knowledge and experience you carry with you? Do you have a suitcase full of statistical assumptions? How many competence bags are there, and what are their names? Do you have suitcases full of real-world experience, or are those bags still empty?

Innovation favors a prepared mind. How prepared are you? Try this checklist:

- Learn creativity techniques through reading, seminars, and conferences.
- Build a network of innovators who will sharpen one another with wit and wisdom.
- Become affiliated with an association that promotes innovation so that you can tap into the latest resources and thinking. One such organization is the Innovation Network founded by Joyce Wycoff. Visit www.thinksmart.com. Another organization is a wonderfully creative group in Australia known as Mindwerx. Visit www.mindwerx.com.au.
- Arrange your filing cabinets based on the laws of association, not linearity.
- Regularly review and simplify the mental structures you cultivate for the purpose of random access.

While we must be prepared for the long haul, we should act quickly when the occasion arises.

Successful innovators have a sense of urgency that drives them to seize the day—*Carpe diem*. Those who get there first become the pioneers, the trailblazers, the pacesetters. In this day and age, it's no longer just the big swallowing the small, but the fast overtaking the slow. The more prepared you are, the more ready you are to seize an opportunity that comes your way before the rest of the pack, and the greater are your chances of achieving a breakthrough.

CAT Nip

My friend Gordy, formerly Gordy the beggar, now Gordy the poet, remembers an early documentary of The Beatles shot during their first tour of the United States. In one scene, a downtown hotel setting, John Lennon sat alone on a couch and was playing a set of pan flutes quietly to himself. Gordy recognized the tune as the opening to the song "Strawberry Fields Forever," a song John Lennon did not write for another three or four years. John carried that interesting riff around in his head until he found a way to marry it to another idea. It was available in the moment.

My Knowledge Files

For much of my life, I have tried to cultivate and organize my knowledge files. I have developed files on leadership, change, creativity, innovation, learning to learn, and writing. I want to share a critical moment that might be useful to a few CATS.

Janell, my wife, and I managed a small business for almost 20 years called the Minnesota Institute for Management Studies (IMS). IMS was created to provide one-day seminars to organization leaders that were equivalent to the executive education you might find at the best universities. We did it in a one-day format with the same faculty.

During those IMS years, I was also actively involved in teaching MBA students. Being someone who is always looking for ways to use what is happening in one part of my life in another part of my life, IMS provided a way to enhance my lectures as a business school teacher, so I attended all the lectures and took extensive notes, in Mind Map form, of course. The years passed, and my Mind Maps became quite extensive, but with each new lecture on change, I added fewer and fewer branches.

Then something interesting happened. The body of knowledge began to shrink. It began to move from complex to simple. Branches were merged, and core themes became more obvious. Once I found the simplicity inside the complexity of one subject, I began looking for it in all that I did. My knowledge files became elegant and more available. I now believe this can happen in any field when you reach the level of mastery.

The point about innovation from this example is straightforward: When you have immediate access to your knowledge, it is available to you in real-time interactions with others. When your knowledge rubs up against someone else's knowledge and the fur flies, you can experience an innovation moment.

Claim Your Pitch

The theme of the book *Top Performer* is that street performers can teach us a great deal about natural energy, the energy present in any authentic human interaction and absent in false, scripted, or controlled situations. The best street performers, Top Performers®, understand the importance of engaging their audience in a way that releases energy. A critical part of what a Top Performer does we have called Claim Your Pitch®.*

The pitch is the place the street performer performs as well as the presence she conveys while occupying that space. The innovator can learn significant lessons from street performers because a powerful claim can silence the voices and still the noise. When I think of a powerful claim, I immediately see Stanislaw Skrowaczewski in my mind.

My grandchildren have a famous and talented grandfather, not me. Their grandfather has conducted in places such as the Sydney Opera House. His music has been nominated for a Pulitzer Prize. At the age of 82, he accepted the job of conductor for the Japanese Symphony. At the age of 84, he extended the contract for two more years. He is clearly a remarkable man.

---

*There are a number of terms that have been registered as a part of the Top Performer intellectual property. Rather than break the flow of the text, I will simply list them here: Claim Your Pitch, Juice the Jam®, Natural Energy®, Mine the Mess®, and Innovation at the Point of Contact® are all registered trademarks of Ontend Creative Partners®.

When Stan approaches the podium, he jogs. When he reaches his perch, he leaps. And when he raises his baton, there is total silence and total concentration by the orchestra and the audience. He exudes a sense of dramatic confidence. There is no doubt that he is going to give the performance every ounce of his energy. Now *that* is a powerful claim and a great example of Claiming Your Pitch.

To Claim Your Pitch as an innovator, you need to show up with clarity and confidence. By *clarity*, I mean that you clearly understand the issue or challenge for which you are seeking an innovation. Confidence is expressed by a powerful claim.

Claim Your Pitch Summary

- **The pitch is the place where a CAT takes a stand and the attitude the CAT brings with him.**
- **CATS choose their pitch with confidence.**
- **CATS feel a sense of ownership for their pitch. That ownership allows them to "see" things they would not otherwise see.**
- **When a CAT chooses to claim her pitch, the clutter and commotion around her are transformed from disruption and distraction into inspiration, focus, and opportunity.**

What is your pitch, and how powerful is your claim?

Ask Why? Now Ask Why Again

One important part of preparation is tightly defining the problem or opportunity. I remember that my friend Jerry McNellis used to start his highly practical innovation process, Compression Planning®, by asking the question "Why?" five times. By the fifth time, the problem or opportunity that needed innovation was clearly described, and there was a shared understanding of the context within which Compression Planning would operate.

CAT Nip

What are the names of the primary content files you have accumulated? For example, you might have files for management, motivation, research design, metallurgy, leadership, astronomy, physics, math, change, the renaissance, or prehistoric fish. Name yours.

- Do you have a Mind Map for each of these? Make one, and keep it updated for the rest of your life.
- Prepare a place to keep neat ideas?
- Review your Mind Maps each week? Do it.

A CAT'S Eye View of Life 2

When I bought my first new family car, it was a Volkswagan Squareback. I hadn't noticed many of them on the road, so it felt sort of, well, special. Over the next few weeks, I saw Squarebacks everywhere. *Did they multiply overnight?* In reality, the only thing that had changed was that the

Squareback had become personal. I had an emotional connection to the car that heightened my senses. I now could "see" cars that had been invisible to me. This is why preparing to innovate is so important. It helps us "see" helpful ideas and concepts in a cluttered world. It sharpens our attention.

LIFE 3

CATS Know that Innovation Isn't Normal

We must understand the tight protective grip of the norm in order to appreciate the methods of escape.

You may have heard the phrase, "Fish discover water last." If you understand what this means, you are well on your way to living the third life of innovation. We humans are for the most part normal, and normal for us is like the water in which a fish lives its entire life. It is all around us, and we never give it a thought. Innovation, however, requires us to get outside the norm.

As CATS, we need to fully understand this powerful force called *normal* in order to appreciate how it can both help and hinder innovation. We have already talked about the role of boxes in our life and how to escape from those boxes when we so choose.

Routines

The development of a routine is a physical manifestation in the brain. As you become comfortable with the routine, perhaps even depend on it, it becomes more prominent, and when success depends on violating the routine, you will find yourself drawn to the same old way.

Imagine the life of a cave dweller. Most of the day was spent hunting and gathering in a dangerous and often hostile environment. Let's suppose that in that environment the animals made distinctive sounds, and the sound of the man-eating slug was *umpa umpa*. Further, suppose there were hundreds of sounds, each clearly distinguishable from another. The human brain evolved in an associative way so that the sound of *umpa umpa* was immediately connected to the man-eating slug, and flight was instantaneous. If the brain had evolved as a serial-processing mechanism, however, on hearing *umpa umpa*, the cave dweller would have to go through the list of animal sounds until he got a match with the slug sound—by which time he would already have been eaten. The normal brain works by creating associations.

The notion of a slug has an actual associative pathway in the brain, like water running down a deforested hillside. Erosion occurs each time it rains, and the small channels that are shaped by the running water become deeper and deeper. Soon, the rain has but one or two places to accumulate as the channels become crevices in the hillside. So it is with the brain. The process keeps us alive and allows us to function in a world of infinite choices.

These channels are called many things: crevices, memories, routines, boxes, traces, paradigms, or just "the way things are done around here." Every time innovation occurs, it must encounter routines, or it wouldn't be innovation.

Now suppose that our cave dwellers come on a plains tribe of remarkably attractive people. The one glitch is that this tribe uses the sound *umpa umpa* to say, "I love you." Every time a cave dweller falls in love with a plains person, the cave dweller ends up running away. This is not good for a diverse gene pool, and neither is it good for innovation. We need to have techniques to counter the routine, to get far from the norm, to get out of boxes, and to fall in love with a plains person.

Every time innovation occurs, it must encounter routines, or it wouldn't be innovation.

Paradigms

Thomas Kuhn, in a book entitled, *The Structure of Scientific Revolutions*, used the word *paradigm* to refer to old and trusted ways of doing things. Joel Barker and Charthouse International, in the Charthouse Learning film entitled, *The Business of Paradigms*, have brought the concept of a paradigm into the common parlance. The following is a simple paradigm story brought to you compliments of the Lundin family.

Our home in Minnesota is older and only partially air conditioned. When the temperature goes into the 80s, we often use fans. When it hits the 90s, we close up the house and turn on the window air conditioners. When it hits 100, we stick our heads in the freezer. This was an 80-degree day.

After making coffee in the kitchen, I noticed that the fan was making a rather obnoxious sound, a kind of a rattle. I am not known for my mechanical skills, but I decided to accept the challenge of silencing the fan. On closer inspection, I could see that the blade was wobbling, and I concluded that a tightening was needed, so I took off the outer case and turned the knob, which quickly came off in my hand. Yes, it was indeed loose.

For the next 30 minutes I worked on tightening the fan, but I simply couldn't twist it back on. Just after I had decided that it must be hopelessly stripped and turned my attention back to the coffee pot, my wife came into the kitchen. The silly woman started messing with the fan, and I thoughtfully advised her that she was wasting her time and that I had spent 30 minutes working on it and had tried everything imaginable. I suggested strongly that she save her energy because part of the knob must be stripped, and we should toss the fan into the trash. I then went upstairs to write about innovation.

When I came down to refill my coffee cup, I was surprised to find the fan working and no longer making that obnoxious sound. I looked at my wife, who was looking at me with that kind of smile—the kind of smile men hate, if you know what I mean. I asked what happened, and she said, "Well, darling. I am usually the one who cleans the fans, and since I have to remove them clockwise for cleaning, I have learned to tighten them in a counterclockwise fashion."

This embarrassing and often-repeated paradigm story is one that I will never live down. However, it is interesting that it happened at the exact time as I was writing this chapter, providing me with one of the best personal examples that I have of this principle. Was that a coincidence or was I able to "see" the example because I was ready to see it?

Do you have a fan repair story?

The Day I Met the Learning Curve

When I was 49, I discovered the Concept Two rowing machine. I went into the health club, and there it was. I had never seen a rowing machine like it and quickly found someone to show me how to use it. I rowed for a few minutes and went about my usual workout.

A couple of weeks later I noticed a chart on the wall above the rowing machine where people were posting their times for 2,500 meters. I decided to post a score of my own. Since I was running ultra marathons at the time, I was in good shape and posted a decent score. Some of the scores posted were better, and some were worse. "Cool," I thought. And I went to the weight room for some shoulder work.

Later that month the chart had been embellished, and the best times were organized according to age. My time was one of the top times for those 40 to 49 years of age. Since my fiftieth birthday was fast approaching, I looked at the other 50s. None of the times was even close. So I thought, "I wonder how fast I can row 2,500 meters and how competitive I would be if I trained?" One of the great things about the Concept Two is that an international register of best times is organized and made available. There is also a series of regional competitions and an annual championship. I trained hard, made progress, and decided to compete. My times were consistently dropping—the learning-training curve in action. I went to Wisconsin and rowed a personal best, winning the 50s. I went to a local meet and improved my time. Then I then went to Colorado and rowed the worst time in months!

If you believe in the textbook learning curve and something like this happens, you consider giving up. I trained hard and bonked. Why go on? And I actually had thoughts of quitting. But I decided to give it one more try and registered for a competition in Atlanta. In Atlanta, my time was so good that the sponsors paid my way to the international championship. And I had almost given up. Never confuse the learning curve with reality. We have times of recovery. We have setbacks. The only sensible way to proceed when you know the truth about learning and failure is to persist.

This story also would be a good example for Life 7: CATS Say "How Fascinating!"

The Innovation Zone

My friend Mick the Juggler has experienced breakthroughs on the edge. The edge is the boundary between two paradigms. While learning to spin a ball on his finger, he developed a new spinning movement with his yo-yo. When juggling, he frequently would cross his hands, something yo-yo masters never did. He then developed yo-yo tricks that had never been done before because they broke the crossing-hands paradigm.

The implications here are rather straightforward. Learning something new is exciting. Learning and experiencing new things also can take CATS into the innovation zone, where what they have learned provokes them to reconsider and expand on what they already know. CATS see things in a new way in the innovation zone, and the paradigm literature is full of examples.

Associative Boundaries

It is not that someone is more or less creative than you. It is a difference in the strength of your respective associative boundaries.

There are individual differences in the strength of our associative boundaries. Therefore, while the human brain operates according to the law of association, some of us have weak associative boundaries, and that makes it possible for us to consider options outside the norm more easily.

In our day-to-day lives, we might label someone with strong associative boundaries as being *literal*. Someone with weak associative boundaries might be described as *creative* or *innovative*. The truth is that we are all capable of amazing creativity, but there are individual differences in our associative boundaries.

Thus, if someone says to you, "Wow, you are really creative. Your mind moves all over the place with ease," the humble response would be, "Aw shucks, I just have weak associative boundaries."

CAT Nip

Consider putting yourself in situations that will stretch your boundaries:

- Travel, but without a tour group. Have a personal experience.
- Read biographies of people in a variety of fields.
- Hang out with those who are not at all like you.
- Observe life!
- Try things just for the sake of experiencing them (legal things).
- Look for ways to walk in someone else's shoes.

N-Dimensional Semantic Space and Associations

Because this point is so crucial, I will use one more example. I had a professor of psychology who used and relished using the concept of *N*-dimensional semantic space. To this day, I am not really sure what he meant, but I think it had to do with every word and its correlation with all other words as the number of words went to *N*. Use this phrase sometime at a cocktail party, and enjoy the blank stares.

Back to the point: Words have correlations with other words. When I say *black*, there is a high probability that you will say *white*. This is a strong association in most minds. However, if I say *black* and you say *night*, you may in fact be demonstrating that you have weak associative boundaries. Try it sometime. Ask 10 people to give you their first response to words *black*, *up*, *rose*, *in*, and *tiger*. Most of the answers will be *white*, *down*, *red*, *out*, and *Woods*. These are strong associations. If you get other words, you may have identified someone with weaker associative boundaries, someone comfortable stepping away from the expected and common as a part of her nature.

A CAT'S Eye View of Life 3

Allen Fahden did not have a publisher, so he printed 10,000 copies of his new book, *Innovation on Demand*, on his own. This left him with no money for publicity. Being an innovative type, he took advantage of normal and violated our sense of what a normal bookstore should be. Allen Fahden opened a one-book bookstore.

Big bookstores have many departments, so Fahden's one-book bookstore had many departments. He placed copies of his one book in 13 different departments: art, architecture, anthropology, psychology/self-help, business, sports, religion, travel, philosophy, humor, technology, law, and fiction and literature.

Big bookstores have liberal return policies and customer service, so Fahden's had a liberal return policy: "If for any reason you are not completely satisfied with your book, it will be cheerfully exchanged for any other book in the store—your choice."

While he had no money for marketing, the approach, which violated what we consider normal, generated a lot of publicity. From network TV in the United States and Europe, including ABC News and the BBC, to National Public Radio, and features in numerous major market newspapers, the READdundant Bookstore, that is what he named it, became a phenomenon.

Introduction to the Three Provocations That Allow You to Escape the Norm

To escape the power of the norm, provocations are required. It works this way: The brain is a nest of associations, and those associations have a physical presence. The more an association is used, the stronger it becomes. It's not that you don't want to be creative. Will has nothing to do with it. You are wired to repeat common paths in thinking and in action. Just imagine driving a car if each and every action required independent action as if it were the first time. You would never get out of the garage. Routines provide an important efficiency and security. Both are important values.

So it takes a provocation to remove you from your well-ingrained ways of thinking. And once you have escaped from the norm with the help of a provocation, you have the opportunity to see other options, other ways of doing things, and other ways of thinking, and some of these will look like they might work or are in other ways interesting.

Your brain will see the potentially useful ideas and make the connection instantaneously.

The next three lives introduce you to three types of provocation. *Physical provocations* come from objects, written descriptions, and assaults on the senses, but not words spoken by another human being. The words of people with whom one is conversing provide a *social provocation*. It is not just the words that provoke but also the presence of a personality with emotions and beliefs. Brainstorming would be the best example of social provocation. Asking thoughtful and pointed questions would be another. *Intellectual provocation* is a result of playing games with the mind. Using opposites, random words, and logical impossibilities for the sole purpose of provoking novel thoughts would be three examples of intellectual provocation. Most humor is a result of an intellectual provocation.

It is true that both physical and intellectual provocations can precede or accompany social provocation. Such a combination frequently makes sense. While I don't think it is important to classify every possible provocation, it is important to note that provocations can come from things, from people, and from intellectual stimulants.

LIFE 4

CATS Welcome Physical Provocation

"That is fascinating stuff. Look at the odd way it reacts. You say it is an energy-absorbing material. What if we . . . ?"

"Have you looked at the new insurance product just released by our rival? What if we . . . ?"

Life 4 is about real provocation. When something primarily physical, like the beak of a finch (Darwin's theory of evolution), or some sticky stuff that almost works (3M), or a collection of neat stuff (IDEO tech box) is the provocation for an innovation, I call it *physical provocation*. Even toys on the conference room table can be of value as a provocation. In this section we look at a variety of physical provocations.

A Strategic Break Is When the Work Gets Done

While in my last year of graduate school a number of events conspired to take me into the world of commerce rather than the world of academia, and I became a partner in a consulting firm. The focus of our firm was the new field of educational program evaluation that just happened to be the subject of my dissertation. I soon found myself immersed in this growing startup and working long hours to provide a steady flow of new business.

To win the business in this emerging field, you had to first write a proposal. For small bits and pieces of business, the proposal could be routine, but when competing for larger contracts, your proposal needed to stand out. I often would find myself at my desk struggling to find a unique twist that would catch the client's eye and put our proposal in a favorable position. One day I was just not finding any inspiration, and out of frustration, I went for a jog.

About the time I broke into a sweat, I had completely forgotten the proposal, and I was into the run. It was then that the ideas started flowing, and by the time I returned home, I had a couple of great ways to be innovative in my presentation.

After that, I would purposefully use running as a way to generate those important innovative ideas, and it always worked. At the point that I was totally into the run and not thinking about work at all, the ideas would start popping up. I guess the subconscious was simply waiting for some space, and when that spaciousness was provided, it went to work.

This is why I say a break is a chance for the work to get done—the important innovative work, I should add.

Thomas Edison Went Fishing*

Thomas Edison knew well the importance of spaciousness as a physical provocation. He would

---

*It would be reasonable to ask why this example and the Lundin jogging break aren't found in Life 1 as examples of reducing the clutter. The answer is that, in both these examples, spaciousness is consciously used as a provocation. It is, however, a close call. And both examples, in the grand scheme of things, are rather unimportant.

sit at the end of the dock at his Florida waterfront office with a fishing pole and his line in the water. He never had bait on the hook because to catch a fish would have been a distraction. But he knew that if people thought he was fishing, they would leave him alone, and the ideas would have the spaciousness they needed to appear.

The Bridge Collapse

In 2007, a bridge collapsed in Minneapolis, Minnesota. It was a tragedy that struck a chord around the world because a large portion of the world's population regularly uses a bridge, and you just don't think about safety until something like this happens.

It was estimated that 250,000 people passed over the bridge every day. It was the most traveled bridge in Minnesota. All those people had to find a new way to work. *The bridge collapse provided a real provocation that forced 250,000 people out of their routine.* Many routes were discovered, some of which were shorter, some of which were more interesting, and some of which went by a great coffee shop. Being forced out of a routine resulted in a lot of discoveries as people went through neighborhoods they had never seen, by shops and restaurants that looked interesting, and past houses that looked appealing. Some of the discoveries were useful and became a new part of a life or lifestyle. It began with a physical provocation.

A Physical Provocation Collection

At IDEO, the physical provocation collection is called the *tech box*. This box mostly contains physical objects used by IDEO when in the process of creating innovative products. When people are focused on products for the physical world, odd bits and pieces can be enormously provocative. When people are working on services, the provocations might differ. I watched the general manager, Tom Kelley, go through the tech box one day: drawers bursting with interesting objects provided him with plenty to discuss.

It became clear that the box contained "neat stuff" and that the neat stuff was used to stimulate thinking and provoke ideas. Team members often would bring neat stuff to brainstorming sessions. These brainstorming sessions are to IDEO what water is to fish. Saying that team members do brainstorming would be misleading because it is much more than that. At IDEO, brainstorming is very much a part of who the people are; it is a constant. And being sought after to attend a brainstormer is a large compliment. The neat stuff brings physical provocation into the brainstormers and makes them richer.

A Neat Stuff Collection

Any business that cares about innovation should have a neat stuff collection. Use your imagination. What sort of neat stuff would be provocative in your company's discussions about new products or services? What sorts of things would trigger a few new connections in a discussion? How will you decide what neat stuff should be immortalized in the container, and what won't make the cut? How will you decide when some neat stuff will replace other neat stuff? The following are examples of neat stuff that you might include in your collection:

- A strange material
- A strange design
- A kids' game
- A picture of an underground mall
- A story about Dubai
- A powerful metaphor
- A stimulating story
- Something that breaks the rules
- A 10-year-old newspaper
- A collection of award-winning print ads
- A concert program that stands out
- A coffee table book about cats
- Pictures of customers using a product

CAT Nip

What would be in your neat stuff collection?

An Organizational Example

For a number of years, I cotaught an executive MBA class with Larry Horsch, a venture capitalist who served as chairman of the board of one of his ventures, SciMed Life Systems, during a time when it needed more funding on six different occasions and then became a career-making success. SciMed, a medical device company, merged with Boston Scientific during the time Larry and I taught together, and although Boston Scientific was the larger firm, many of the SciMed Life people took key leadership roles. Larry had a lot of stories, and I was fascinated by his view of a world I saw only from a distance. I will never forget the story I am about to share because it is such a great innovation story and because, over the years, I heard it often.

After years of struggling, SciMed found itself in the angioplasty market with a product. The company was not alone and had larger competitors with deep pockets. In order to emerge a winner, the company had to be quicker and more agile. A tension—a classic tension at that—existed between research and marketing. Research always wanted more time, and marketing—in the eyes of research—wanted to run with products before they were ready. Each department was suspicious of the other's motives.

The president of SciMed decided to tackle this problem head on and physically placed marketing in the center of the research department.

The greater understanding that developed from this physical arrangement allowed SciMed to increase its speed to market with high-quality products and become a darling of Wall Street.

Tragedy as a Provocation

I was in Toowoomba, a city two hours from Brisbane, Australia, and was preparing for a lunchtime talk. My host was loquacious, and I have to admit that I was listening with only half an ear. Then something he said caught my full attention. My event was his second event of the day, and he was describing the Queenslander of the Year award ceremony that took place in the morning. He outlined the tragic story of the winner and described how the tragedy became a provocation for something good. The following is the press release that describes Brian Egan's story.

The Queensland Senior Australian of the Year 2008 Is Drought Relief Helper Brian Egan

Brian Egan knows exactly what drought-stricken families are going through—he lost his own farm in the 1990s due to drought and personal depression. Five years ago he and his wife, Nerida, established Aussie Helpers to try to alleviate hardship and lift the spirits of families severely affected by drought. By tapping into the bush telegraph, Aussie Helpers finds farming families who are in desperate need of assistance. Brian and his band of committed volunteers have

given away more than 150 tonnes of groceries, over 600 tonnes of stock feed and assisted more than 1,000 families. Aussie Helpers raises funds through thrift shops in Dalby and Charleville and through donations to the annual Bush Christmas Appeal and the ongoing Drought Relief Appeal. Brian's helpers help transform Christmas from a bleak and depressing time to one of joy and celebration, while other money goes toward farm repairs, dental care and coastal holidays for outback families.

This is an inspiring story but incomplete. Here is the rest of the story. Brian Egan became so depressed by his loss that he considered taking his own life. At the low point in his life, he found himself talking to a counselor. The counselor was a former priest who had left the church and went into counseling. He listened to Brian's tale of woe and said to Brian, "There is only one thing you can do that will pull you out of your depression. Find somebody worse off than you are and help them." The preceding story describes some of what Brian did. Not included is his work with youth and other related ventures.

The Brian Egan story highlights innovation provoked by tragedy. And any tragedy is both a physical provocation (an unexpected event) and a social provocation (it provokes emotions and conversations). Brian was physically provoked when he lost his farm. Brian then was socially provoked by the counselor. Stories such as Brian's are common. Tragedy provokes a novel response that makes the world a better place.

On losing her sister to a drunk driver, Melanie Lundin organized a program on the Santa Clara campus called "Cabs on Campus" to be sure every student out drinking, something college students do occasionally, has a ride home. Melissa Lundin was provoked to think of new ways to raise money for Gilda's Club, a nonmedical place for those with cancer and their families to hang out and get support.

CAT Nip

The following are some ways to physically provoke yourself using the naturally occurring opportunities that life has to offer:

- Volunteer to help in a playschool. Watching kids at play can be such an inspiration. They say and do the most wonderful things in their innocence, and it's always refreshing.
- Listen to types of music that you're not attuned to.
- Take up a new sport or hobby to broaden your horizon. You'll meet new friends and have a range of new experiences.
- Chill out with your teenage kids. Put evaluation and judgement aside, and just be there. There is much we can learn from their radical overtures and "no fear" outlook.
- Go on a holiday that offers a completely different experience from your previous vacations. If you are a typical city hopper, try a quiet sojourn in the mountains. If you are the die-hard sun-and-sea vacationer,

head for the theme parks. Try camping out under the starry skies. Go to exotic places off the beaten track.

- Travel to places where people do things differently.
- Do someone else's job for a day. If you can't do her job, try to walk in her shoes by shadowing her.
- Really experience another culture as an adult; this means forget the tour guide and engage the people and the culture.
- Buy season tickets to a comedy club.
- Read books on subjects that have no obvious practical value.
- Learn a new language, or at least learn more than words for toilet and "would you like to see my etchings."
- Sign up for a cooking class that teaches cuisine from a different culture.
- Pick up a skill with which to entertain your friends, such as juggling, clowning, ventriloquism, or card tricks.
- Read *MAD* magazine. Read comics.
- Walk in the woods without a note pad.
- Train your dog so that it is qualified to visit nursing homes and homes for displaced children.
- Teach a physically handicapped child to swim.
- Decide that on Friday you are going to be of service to as many people as possible, and do it.
- Make this list your "bucket list."

A CAT'S Eye View of Life 4

A butcher outside Florence who is also known as a remarkable Tuscan chef honors and respects the animals he prepares for consumption. One day he was thinking about conservation while he was working in his shop. In a moment of insight, he saw the carcass differently as these two thought streams collided. He realized that there are small amounts of meat that rarely get used as food. An idea emerged as conservation and respect for animals connected: Why not find ways to prepare the cow meat that is usually wasted, specifically the meat from around the knees. He began experimenting with different approaches to preparing and seasoning this meat. He now serves delicious dishes in the restaurant above his butcher shop, dishes that use the meat that once went to waste. I have eaten these dishes and can verify their tastiness.

LIFE 5

CATS Enjoy Social Provocation

"What you just said made me think of. . . . ."

A close relative to physical provocation is social provocation. Physical provocation is provocation by an object, a condition of the real world, the way things are arranged, or the senses. Social provocation comes from the interaction with other human beings. Brainstorming, while often misunderstood, is easily the best-known and most commonly used innovation technique. Brainstorming is a form of social provocation.

Social provocation is different from intellectual provocation. Intellectual provocation is the provocation that comes from challenging your thinking. It can be done individually or in groups, whereas social provocation requires conversation.

Human interaction is a great source of innovative ideas because of its spontaneous nature. In everyday situations, it is hard to predict how another person will respond to what we say. Unusual and contentious responses are always provocative and can lead to an unexpected insight.

We have all experienced the phenomenon of intense creative conversation—a conversation where the sparks were flying. The sparks we are referring to are the many ideas that emerged while we were engaged in passionate conversation. What we were experiencing is what I call *social provocation.*

Human interactions can be a powerful source of innovation. Exibit A is brainstorming, a technique about which we all have some understanding and that is often misunderstood.

Brainstorming

Brainstorming is most people's first response when asked about innovation techniques with which they are familiar. In organizations, brainstorming can be an annual event or, as in the case of organizations such as IDEO, a part of daily life as common as a coffee break. In a "brainstormer" (as IDEO calls a brainstorming event), the spontaneous and novel nature of human interaction is maximized by making the unique responses of different individuals highly desirable within a framework of guidelines.

It is important to remember that the purpose of brainstorming is provocation and that the rules that often accompany a brainstorming session are meant to ensure the primacy of the desired result—ideas.

At any given time of day, somewhere in the world there is a group engaged in brainstorming for ideas to solve a problem or identify an opportunity. The rules that guide the sessions vary, the use of the results may vary, the enthusiasm of the participants varies, but one thing is common: these groups are using social provocation to generate ideas.

Alex Osborn is given credit for coining the term *brainstorming*, and IDEO is frequently mentioned because of the way the company has made brainstorming a part of its unique culture of innovation.

Osborn's 1950s classic, *Applied Imagination*, made the following statement: "Creativity comes from a blend of individual and collective 'ideation.'"

Osborn supplied some ground rules to keep us from being too human because human beings are quick to criticize. It is in our nature. Every list of ground rules I have seen, over 30 lists researching for this book, use some variation of these rules. I am going to comment on brainstorming in general and then present the four most common guidelines.

General Comments about the Research on Brainstorming

Research shows that group brainstorming is less effective than individual brainstorming when the quantity of ideas is the measure. The finding that the group is less effective than the sum total of individuals is not too surprising because you can't talk and listen at the same time, and you can't all talk at once. It is also true that there are lazy or shy people who will keep a low profile in a group, something they can't do alone.

Research also shows that when the quantity goes up, the quality also goes up. The more ideas identified, the more *good* ideas identified. I will accept this finding, but I must admit I find the criteria for quality a bit hard to understand.

Most practitioners use a combination of individual and group brainstorming. This seems like a good strategy. Some practitioners use a combination of divergence, convergence, divergence, and then convergence. Compression Planning is one such system. This means that you get as many ideas as possible during a set time. Then you analyze, combine, and eliminate ideas. Next, you tighten the problem statement and brainstorm again, followed by a final evaluation of findings. I have been in these sessions with the grand master of compression planning, Jerry McNellis, and I find them highly productive and extremely practical.

To me, the research findings are useful but incomplete. A place such as IDEO causes me to look more closely and ask a series of questions:

- Was participation voluntary?
- Were a number of perspectives represented?
- Was the problem tightly defined?
- Did the participants understand the power of the norm and the role of provocation?

Brainstorming Rules

1. **Do not criticize another person's ideas during the brainstorming session.**
   - **Criticism will reduce participation and limit scope.**
   - **All ideas are equal at the time they are produced.**
2. **Try to avoid self-censorship; say whatever comes to mind.**

- **This is internal criticism.**

3. **Generate as many ideas as possible in the time allowed.**
    - **This assumes that quantity is more important than quality because when quantity goes up, so will quality.**
4. **Build on the ideas of others.**
    - **Central to social provocation is one person being provoked by another.**
    - **When well facilitated, this approach can lead to higher-quality ideas.**
5. **Don't bother with brainstorming in a toxic environment.**

CAT Pause

Are the brainstorming sessions you attend actually dedicated to innovation? Is there a set of guidelines?

The Medici Effect

I was in Florence with my wife in April of 2008. We traveled with the poet David Whyte and 30 others who also found David's poetry and his vision of foreign travel as an authentic endeavor and a collaborative event intriguing. In the mornings and evenings, we would converse. In the afternoons, we walked the hills of Tuscany. One evening we sat in an old monastery in the hills of Tuscany and listened to an impassioned lecture about the role of Florence in the Renaissance given by a local professor.

It was in Florence, in the fifteenth century, that Galileo, da Vinci, Machiavelli, and others came to live while pursuing their particular passions. This was made possible by the sponsorship of wealthy benefactors. The best known of these sponsors was the Medici family. It is for that reason Johansson titled his book, *The Medici Effect*. It could have been called "The Renaissance Effect" or "The Tuscany Effect," but since his title exists, I will forgo the ego satisfaction of coming up with my own label and use his to describe an important aspect of provocation.

With so much talent in one place, something happened that would not have been possible had the distances been greater. These individuals and the disciplines they represented rubbed up against one another. They talked, hung out, shared meals, argued, and otherwise connected. These connections between and among painters, sculptors, astronomers, writers, and a host of other artists and scientists led to innovations that would not have occurred were it not for the provocations provided by the close proximity (i.e., physical provocation) and the interaction (i.e., social provocation). It is this interaction at the boundaries of different disciplines and ways of thinking that constitutes the Medici Effect.

Earl Bakken and Social Provocation

In the modern world, a place of great potential for interaction across disciplines is the organization. Near the University of Minnesota, there is an organization known as Abbott Northwestern Hospital. It was at this hospital that two disciplines rubbed up against one another to great effect. The disciplines were electrical engineering and medicine.

Earl Bakken, the man who cofounded Medtronic in 1949, had enjoyed building robots and playing with electricity as a young man. It is reported that seeing the movie *Frankenstein* at the age of eight stimulated his interest in anything electronic. After finishing his schooling, he set up a business that specialized in what he enjoyed most—fixing things electronic. For this reason, he began making routine visits to the Northwestern Hospital. There was always something to fix because electronics had found its way into medicine. Since he was really good at fixing things, the range of things he was asked to fix grew, along with his reputation. His small business of fixing things was operated out of a small garage in Minneapolis. He called it *Medtronic*.

The company repaired televisions and radios and sold some medical equipment. The doctors at the hospital were using more and more electrical equipment, and Earl was often called on to make sure it worked. Eventually, Bakken was asked to be present during surgery in case any of this new equipment failed. If the power went out back in the 1940s and 1950s, the loss of electricity could be profound. And that's just what happened one day, back in 1957. A huge power outage hit Minnesota and Wisconsin, and a giant electrical pacemaker quit working. The child it was keeping alive died.

Bakken was deeply affected by the child's death and didn't need any additional motivation when doctors asked him if there was anything he could develop to help should another blackout occur; he got to work. Provoked by a metronome, the electrical pacemaker, and the death of a child, he developed the first battery-powered pacemaker. After trying it on a dog and seeing that it worked, the doctors used the device on a child. The child lived.

Bakken later described his feelings this way: "I think my proudest moment was seeing that first pacemaker work on a child. That was such an emotional thing for my life. We stopped doing all the other things after that, and we said we're going to concentrate on the pacemaker."

The pacemaker eventually moved inside the body, and Medtronic moved out into the world. The Twin Cities became the epicenter of medical product innovation. Right now, somewhere in the world, a pacemaker is saving or sustaining a life. The provocation that started at the intersection of two electronics and medicine led to an innovation that led to an industry that changed the world. *All innovation is personal. All innovation is the result of personal provocations. Some of those provocations are social.*

Think about the Bakken story and the way the Medicci effect came into play at the boundary between two disciplines.

IDEO and Social Provocation

IDEO is generally accepted as the "gold standard" of brainstorming. My observations would support this designation. At IDEO, though, there are some subtleties that deserve special attention.

The Medicci effect is alive and well at IDEO because brainstormers (brainstorming sessions) are populated by people from a wide variety of disciplines, including designers, linguists, sociologists, anthropologists, builders, psychologists, artists, and managers. This array of disciplines guarantees the opportunity for innovative ideas at the boundaries.

At IDEO, you get *invited* to a brainstormer based on your past contributions, and it is a high honor to be in demand as a participant. It is understood that skill in brainstorming has a normal distribution curve. Some people simply do not function well in groups and are better off doing independent work. Others are so good at brainstorming that they are in constant demand. This is as it should be; working from strengths.

It also should be noted that participants in brainstormers at IDEO often will bring physical objects to a brainstormer, even if there is only a glimmer of connection to the topic. This is done to provoke ideas. Often these objects come from the tech box described in Life 4: Physical Provocation.

Innovation at the Point of Contact

This may be surprising to you, but if you add up all of innovation, I would estimate that 99 percent of it would be innovation at the point of contact. The *point of contact* is the place where two human beings connect. And it is the one place where a company can gain an advantage over the competition. Since innovation at the point of contact is so ubiquitous, it never gets mentioned. That omission stops here! Innovation at the point of contact operates according to the same principles as any other form of innovation. And the point of contact is a great place to explore these principles. You have hundreds of opportunities daily unless you live alone in a cave.

The point of contact is where people interact. Every interaction can be viewed as a provocation. For many organizations, what happens at the point of contact is important to organizational well-being. Whether the organization is a service organization or a provider of products, what happens at the point of contact affects all the following:

- The brand
- The reputation of the organization
- Continued business
- Retention of employees
- Recruitment of employees
- Leadership
- Management
- Customer service
- Quality

- Mind share
- Vision
- Strategy

Experience Zones

A hotel has a number of *experience zones* where there is a greater density of contacts ripe for innovation. When a customer enters a property, she will check in at the front desk. This is a point of contact, and this type of contact is repeated over and over throughout the day. The front desk is a primary experience zone.

If the customer goes to breakfast, she will likely encounter a food service person. If she checks out in person, she will experience another point of contact. And perhaps she will encounter housekeeping or maintenance. Each point of contact is a part of the human experience, and the sum of all those moments, along with the physical experience, adds up to an individual's valuation of the brand. And the valuation will determine repeat business and the quality of the comments made to others when the customer talks about the brand. Every service-oriented organization, whether profit making, nonprofit, or government, has experience zones where reputations are formed one experience at a time.

The innovation at the point of contact is the authentic personal connection. *Authentic* means that the interaction takes a form that is unique to the person engaged. It has an integrity that is present when you treat another as an individual, not as a member of a group. The customer is not an object toward whom you direct a script but an individual with whom you have a real conversation.

The social provocation needed for innovation is always present in the form of another person's words, expressions, and deeds during the interaction. The use of these social provocations to create a unique and personal connection with the customer is perhaps the most underutilized asset in the service industry. And it is free, readily available, and the source of a true competitive advantage if you have a few CATS around.

Juice the Jam®: Lessons on Social Provocation from Street Performers

So how do you get better at this form of innovation? One way is to study masters, and the street performers that Carr Hagerman and I wrote about and filmed in *Top Performer* are great models. They know how to Juice the Jam.

A *jam* is anything that happens unexpectedly—anything that isn't scripted or planned and doesn't have a ready solution or obvious response. Unlike a *mess*, which is stationary and inert, a jam is active and inflicts itself on the performer and the audience and commands attention.

The *juice* is the energy that is extracted when the jam is embraced and used to further the performance. Anne Bogart and Tina Landau, two theater directors who've written a book about a particular form of theater training called *Viewpoints*, capture what it means to look beyond the script and structure to see the juice as an act of discovery. "Of course, a project needs structure and a sense of direction, but can the [performer] aim for *discovery* rather than staging a replica of what has always happened before? Can we resist proclaiming "What it is" long enough to authentically ask, "What is it?"

Juicing the Jam starts with "What is it?" The performer doesn't ignore the disruption but uses it as fuel. Bogart and Landau go on to say that it's about letting something occur rather than making something occur. "The source for action and invention comes to us from others and from the physical world around us."

As we develop our skills at dealing with breakdown, hecklers, and objections, it "leads to greater awareness, which leads to greater choice, which leads to greater freedom." Top Performers have learned that there is great freedom in not worrying about the jams and shifting awareness to the great possibilities embedded within those jams. We, as Top Performers, don't have to chase after everything; we can simply allow more things to *come to us*.

The seeds for our best work often come in the way we work with a jam. Top Performers learn from each jam and the juice they extract from the exchange. A similar jam is often captured and used more confidently at a later time. We learn from our jams. A jam may not have an obvious outcome, but when we step toward it with curiosity, we often find what we need.

In *Trust the Process*, a wonderful book on artistic expression and creativity, author Shaun McNiff writes about the unexpected and the unplanned. He says, "There is no magic unless unplanned expressions arrive to infuse the performance with spontaneous vitality that can never be preconceived"

Top Performers always keep their eye on the crowd. They face the audience as a way to avoid getting lost in the routine or a gag. They know that something interesting could happen at any moment. And they know that they don't know where it will happen or what form it will take, but they intend to see it when it happens. The best performers have amazing face-to-face contact, and they notice everything that's happening.

There are volumes written for the business audience on how to control what happens in our presentations and in our exchanges with customers and clients. You can find dozens of books that lay out a plan for handling the jams that eventually show up in every pitch, whether it is an office, a counter, a sales setting, or a patient encounter in a hospital. No matter how many books and papers we may read about how to deal with each kind of jam, though, only direct experience will teach us how to juice it.

Jams can happen whether we are with people or are working alone. Whether an engineer, a designer, an architect, a writer, or any of the hundreds of other jobs in this virtual world where people find themselves mostly alone, we all encounter the unexpected breakdowns and blocks. The Top

Performer in any field recognizes that everything that happens is material for life, a potential source of energy, and a possible location where innovation lurks and Juices the Jam.

Juice the Jam

- **A *jam* is the uncontrolled and unexpected—it can be anything that happens without warning when one or more human beings are assembled.**
- **CATS welcome a jam because it provides a source of novelty and provocation, and novelty and provocation always produce a burst of natural energy—the *juice*.**
- **Hence the juice is in the jam.**
- **This juice is what keeps CATS full of energy.**
- **The juice is usually natural energy.**
- **You must engage the jam in order to access the energy.**
- **Every jam is different.**
- **The rewards are huge when you skillfully handle a jam.**
- **The jam is a welcome provocation for CATS and an opportunity to innovate.**
- **CAT Wranglers encourage the use of naturally occurring provocations.**

The Experimental Schools Program

Fresh out of college, I cofounded a research and evaluation company. The company would bid on the evaluation portion of government-funded projects in the United States. Our research was designed to show the impact or lack of impact of the program being funded by the government and evaluated by us. Psychologists, statisticians, and measurement specialists usually staffed evaluation studies.

There were a lot of firms bidding on evaluation business, some 50 times our size. In order to win a large contract, we had to develop an idea that caught the attention of the proposal evaluators. Thus, as I worked on the proposal for the experimental schools evaluation, a multi-million-dollar five-year study, I searched for a novel approach.

As an educational psychologist with a strong statistics and measurement background, my initial ideas contained methods consistent with those fields. They also were common. One day when I could no longer focus, I went out for a run (physical provocation). While on the run, I began thinking about the five-year nature of the program and the fact that the same schools would be studied for the entire time. Psychology breaks things down into smaller parts, I thought. What discipline embraces the whole? And then the word *anthropology* popped into my head.

The team that I eventually fielded contained anthropologists, psychologists, sociologists, and economists. It was one of the first times that anthropologists were used to conduct domestic research. The miniethnographies were delightful. And the approach was novel enough to lead to heated debates at the American Anthropology Association meetings. The interaction of the disciplines sharpened our focus, and the results of the evaluation received less notoriety than the approach. It hadn't been done this way before. Social provocation was built into the fabric of the study.

A CAT'S Eye View of Life 5

Hampton Brands, part of the Hilton Group, is in the hospitality business. The company understands and has benefited from improvements in innovation at the point of contact. The hospitality business is highly competitive. I recently drove 2,000 miles on U.S. highways and noted that hotels were clustered at certain exits. A typical exit would have a Hampton Inn, a Holiday Inn Express, a Best Western, a Fairfield Marriott, and a Ramada. It seems clear that their success is directly correlated with the occupancy rate. So what determines where a person will stay?

Hampton has been and will continue to be innovative in bringing new products and services to their customers. But those innovations, over time, can all be copied. The personal human experiences of guests, however, are much harder to copy. Advertising and product innovation may get you to stop once, but the sum of your experiences at the point of contact likely will determine whether you return. People will drive an extra 40 miles to stay at a Hampton Inn. They "get it." The company understands and practices innovation at the point of contact.

Innovations such as curved shower curtains can gain an advantage for a while, especially for those of us who don't want physical contact with the curtain while taking a shower, but such an advantage doesn't last forever. In fact, many chains now have curved shower curtains. This innovation spread quickly. However, if the product innovation is accompanied by a human experience innovation, the advantage can be sustained.

LIFE 6

CATS Promote Intellectual Provocation

There is nothing quite so mentally stimulating as intellectual provocation.

"What if that cat had wings?" "What if we did the opposite of that?"

Intellectual provocation is being provoked by ideas. It is highly cognitive. "Let's pretend this ran backwards. Let's pretend we had an extra thumb. What if trees had no roots? Let's pretend the opposite were true. What if a service station took care of itself?" All these statements have been used as provocations.

Intellectual provocation is critical because not only are our actions controlled by what we consider normal, but our thinking is as well. We see this every time we laugh at a joke. We react because we are fooled. We anticipate a normal conclusion to a story or description and are surprised when our expectations are violated or when different meanings of a word are manipulated. I heard Edward de Bono tell this joke years ago:

Did you hear about the optometrist who fell into the lens-grinding machine? She made a spectacle of herself.

Or this one:

A nasty and unkempt thief went to jail. A friend visited him, and he had a beautiful woman on his lap. The friend remarked, "I thought this was a place of punishment, but here you are with this woman on your lap." The thief answered, "I am her punishment."

It is appropriate that I quote de Bono because no one can match the contributions made by de Bono to the area of intellectual provocation. He is the grandmaster of intellectual provocation and understands the nature of normal and how it takes something extraordinary to get everyday humans to a place where they have an opportunity to innovate. He believes that if you can take your mind to a place it wouldn't ordinarily go, it will seek to return to the comfort of the ordinary. On its way home, however, it will have a chance to bump into something new or interesting. From the mind of Edward de Bono comes the following powerful mental provocation.

Lateral Thinking

Edward de Bono coined this phrase, and you can now find it in any modern dictionary. The idea had been around for centuries, but by naming it, de Bono empowered us. I think of lateral thinking as thinking that has managed to escape the bonds of normal or routine. When we think about a problem, we often follow a series of logical steps, a little like moving along a logical track. As we move along the track, we pass many great ideas, but we don't see them because they are not contained within our logic train. That is, there is no logical reason to leave the track we are on while it is working. Then we reach the end of the track and still have a problem unsolved—what does a CAT do? Intellectual provocation is the answer.

Mick the Juggler Again

To imagine new tricks, Mick the Juggler uses the provocation of "the opposite." He asks himself, "What would the opposite of this look like?" and then follows his imagination to a new place. For instance, many juggling acts involve members of the audience by passing something to them. Mick asked, "What would happen if the audience passed things to the juggler instead?" He discovered a whole new and highly engaging frontier.

Following are further examples of Mick's imagination at work. In each case, a new trick or routine evolved from the mental provocation. What would happen if you didn't attach the string to your finger? What would happen if the string was not attached to the yo-yo? What if you crossed or twisted the strings? Mick says that questions such as these have led to a lot of his innovations in juggling.

Followership

I had been teaching MBA students and working on my knowledge files for a few years when I had an interesting thought. I was working on leadership, a topic with universal interest at that time that was used to indicate the practices of those in leadership positions. I had grown a bit bored with the incessant clamor for more and more on leadership. It had been my observation that individual employees also could show great leadership skills, even though they were not in leadership positions. I had also noticed that being in a leadership position did not mean that you had leadership skills. But talking about those on the bottom of the organization chart was confusing to others. So one day I said "opposite of leadership," and the word *followership* popped into my head. At the time, it was novel and immediately attracted some interest and a lot of scepticism. Colleagues said, "What could be so difficult about following? It is leadership that really makes a difference. Why waste your time on a subject with absolutely no sex appeal. Leadership is the important subject. You are wasting your time."

Having caught a glimpse of something in that moment of creation, however, I decided to quietly flesh out the idea. For the next two years, I developed the idea, wrote a couple articles, and engaged in a lot of conversations with MBA students about leadership and followership. My followership included a rigorous set of skills, including such things as being "up tough" and "owning the territory." (Today, I might say "having fierce conversations and claiming your pitch.") If you can be in a leadership position and not have leadership skills, I thought, then you certainly could be in a follower position and not have follower skills. It was kind of fun bucking the established way of thinking.

Then one day I learned a big lesson. A book was released entitled, *Followership*. Someone else had captured the market by being first in print with a book. I would have written a very different book but it was too late. I had missed a chance to be first to market with the title. This experience provided another provocation that has served me well: act on your beliefs, or someone else will.

Getting Practical about Intellectual Provocation

Three conditions need to exist in order to maximize intellectual provocation:

1. You have a problem or an opportunity you are working on.
2. You fully engage your repertoire of intellectual innovation tactics that at other times might seem ridiculous, but because you understand the power of the norm and the nature of intellectual provocation, they make sense.
3. You allow yourself to embrace the possibilities, and you look for reasons why they might work versus why they might fail.

There are a number of techniques to get you out of your normal zone, and they can be used alone or with a group. For example:

- Take a random word out of a dictionary or text and play with the possibilities. Let the word pull you into a different idea space, and consider that space with an eye toward discovery.
- Use an opposite to provoke you.

- Use a logical impossibility to provoke you. Frame the impossible statement, "The trash picks itself up," and then discuss whatever is provoked.
- Use a word bounce. One person says a word, and another bounces off that word to a different idea space. When something interesting is provoked, write it down.
- Have someone in your group play the role of fool. Whenever that person says something absurd, consider it.
- If you are working on something that can be stated as a process, list the elements of the process, and remove one or two elements. Let the result serve as your provocation.

CAT Pause

Earlier in this book, in the second challenge in Chapter 2, I cited the example of reverse gear in a car and how it doesn't make sense from a cost standpoint. When you are facing a wall, however, you really need reverse gear. We need to think about intellectual provocation in the same way. It is not very efficient, so you don't use it all the time, just as you don't drive in reverse all day. When you come to the end of a logical sequence and find yourself staring at a dead end, though, mental provocation can help any CAT. Think about the challenges you face, and contemplate whether you might want to use intellectual provocation or a combination of intellectual and social provocation for one of them.

A CAT'S Eye View of Life 6

A large home-supply chain was aware that in order to keep its reputation for being innovative, it needed to regularly come up with new ideas. Groups met to brainstorm for new ideas, but the new ideas were few and far between. One owner sat down at her desk and decided to try a little intellectual provocation. She listed all the basic elements of her store on a sheet of paper. The list included customers, departments, parking lot, employees, checkout, etc. After completing the list, she *intellectually provoked* herself by drawing a line through two of the items on the list. She then began thinking what it would be like without these two ingredients. She found herself considering things that were definitely outside the usual owner brainstorming sessions.

At the next meeting of her colleagues, she offered to hold a discussion about new ideas. She even went as far as inviting specific colleagues who seemed open (weak associative boundaries) to add ideas. She outlined the rules and then introduced the first provocation for discussion using the rules of brainstorming. Group members had one of the wildest sessions in which they had ever participated and came up with dozens of novel ideas. They took those ideas to the whole group for refinement and analysis, and several innovations took shape.

LIFE 7

CATS Say "How Fascinating!"

When you truly embrace how human beings learn, the word *failure* becomes an affirmation.

One of the barriers to innovation is our misunderstanding and fear of failure. It is hard to remember that failure is required for learning when you are standing in the ashes of a business venture gone sour. It is much too philosophical at the point of great pain to remember that risk is a part of any equation that includes rework. So we really have a love-hate relationship with failure. Serial entrepreneurs and scientists usually learn to appreciate the importance of failure in the bigger picture of innovation, whereas others would be hard pressed to say something good about it. So what is a CAT to do?

Failure does not get the respect it deserves as the key ingredient in much of our learning. Have you ever observed that you learn a little from a success and a lot from a failure? So does everyone else! We have long been intrigued by the leadership literature on the importance of working through guided failures so that you know how to respond to something big when you are the boss.

Failure at the Top

Eugene Jennings, an expert in the field of leadership associated with the University of Michigan, was a leading thinker on leadership in the 1980s and had a particularly interesting project. Each year he held a meeting for top executives and their spouses. Nothing new there. To be invited to Eugene's meeting, however, you had to have suffered a serious unexpected failure in your career. This was an unusual gathering—one part healing, the other part research.

I vividly remember my conversations with Eugene as he discussed his findings. He was a spellbinding speaker, but he also had some of the most interesting content that this young entrepreneur and MBA professor had encountered up to that time. Eugene found one common trait among those who reached the top rungs of the ladder and failed: Their record was unblemished. These failed executives ran into their first difficulties at the top with no practice in tough times along the way. And so, when the tough times appeared, they did all the wrong things. They became isolated rather than becoming more open to a variety of inputs. They avoided feedback and withdrew. And when they were fired, they were surprised.

Eugene's was a welcome voice of reason during a time when fast-tracked executives often moved to lofty positions while never spending enough time in any one place to be held accountable. I have never thought about "fast track" in the same way since. If one of the goals in developing executives is to prepare them for tough times as well as sunny days, they will need to know how to handle setbacks. The only way to learn this skill is to make some mistakes and be held accountable for fixing them. Handling failure is a learned skill. And like it or not, all of us will experience our share.

It has been suggested that the same phenomenon may befall students for whom school comes easily and who achieve their top grades without a lot of fuss. They also miss the learning experience that comes with failure and are not well equipped when the big one comes along, as it always does.

How Fascinating!

So what is the appropriate response to failure? Well, I love the work of Tony Buzan. When Tony makes a presentation (and I have seen at least a dozen of his presentations and have participated in a week-long filming of Tony live), he will often juggle as a metaphor for learning. Providing each member of the audience with three tennis balls, he will spend breaks guiding them in the process of learning to juggle. If you want a smile, just think of a conference room full of 200 aspiring jugglers. Some of his students learn to juggle, some don't, some already knew, but all learn how to respond to dropping the ball. As Tony builds his case for "little failures as building blocks for success," he teaches each participant the way to greet a setback. The only rational way is with the response, "How fascinating! What can I learn from this? I will learn what I can, and try, try, try, again."

Understand the Learning Curve

Having the appropriate response to failure requires that you understand the learning curve. The following chart captures the learning curve as seen in the psychology textbooks I studied at university. This is how most people assume learning occurs.

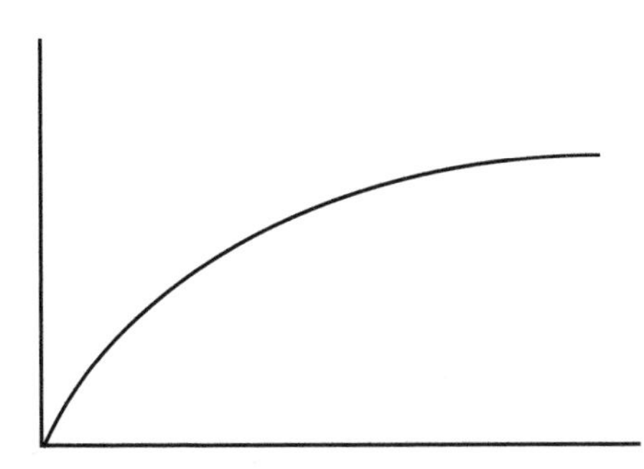

Learning curve as presented in psychology books.

The above curve is created when you summarize the learning of a large number of people. In fact, the chart is an abstraction, not a reality.

However, if you believe that with each trial you should get better and better and better (never slipping backward), then you are applying a metaphor that can only lead to real failure. Eventually, you will not make the progress you expect with your [choose one] guitar lessons, golf game, child rearing, bridge lessons, writing, singing, soccer playing, weightlifting, poetry, flower garden, cattle raising, or sales presentations.

This next chart captures the learning curve as experienced by a regular human being. It goes up and down. Failure is incorporated as part of successful learning.

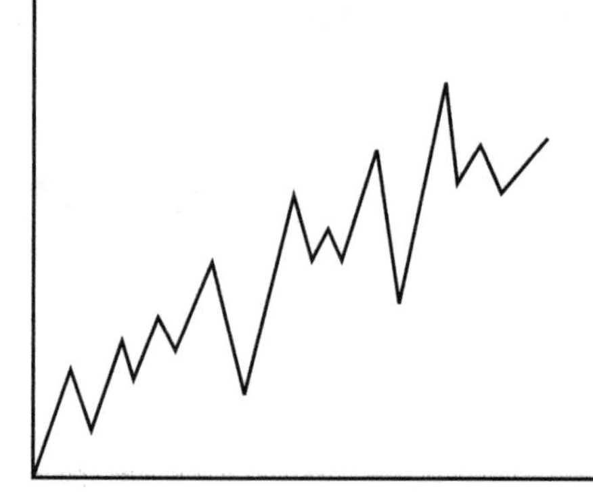

Learning curve as experienced by a person.

Gordy the Poetic Street Performer says this about the learning curve:

I think this is a point that needs to be hammered home. I could have used this advice when I was doing standup comedy in New York. I look back at that time and wish I saw that learning is a peaks-and-valleys experience. When I would have a great show, I was convinced I had arrived. And the next night, if it was a bad show, I thought of myself as an utter failure. If I was better equipped to see the whole journey, I might still be performing standup, and doing well at it.

Multiply this experience by 6 trillion, and you will have the unintended consequence of the learning-curve myth on human beings.

One Last Story about Mick the Juggler

A *diablo* is like a large yo-yo not attached to the string. Mick had worked hard and had taught himself to perform with two diablos at the same time.

This is an extremely difficult trick to learn, and he had gotten pretty good. One day he saw a video from Japan showing a juggler using three diablos. His first reaction was that it was a hoax because he didn't think juggling three diablos was possible. He knew it was possible to doctor video, but he was intrigued enough to check with the source. Sure enough, there were a couple guys in Japan juggling three. Mick decided to learn the trick, and he started the process of learning.

Mick spent, on average, four hours a day for over a year before he mastered the trick. It took that long to develop the muscle memory needed to do something so complex. So what is the point of the story? Can you imagine how many failures were required to achieve success with three diablos? And they had to be good failures as well. If Mick didn't have a "how fascinating" point of view, he would have lost his mind. But he understood that the failures were his only road to success. So he persevered.

Try Starting

One of the great barriers to innovation is procrastination. I want to share a secret: You will never work it all out ahead of time, and you will never eliminate all the risk of failure. Sometimes you just have to start!

In recent times, aspiring writers have asked about my writing. They think I know something. They believe that once they learn my secrets, they can write the book that they have inside of them, and it will be a success. They ask me when I write, where I write, and how I write. I am polite and encouraging, but I know what they are doing. They are trying to work everything out ahead of time. They figure they can't fail if they work everything out before they start. And after listening patiently, I give them the best advice I have:

"*Writers, write.* That is what writers do. You must write to get better at writing. You will never know ahead of time what the outcome will be because you are engaged in an act of discovery. I do know one thing for sure. In order to have a chance at becoming a successful writer, whatever that means to you, you must first write. Take the first step now. Start writing."

Courage is not the absence of fear.

Courage is taking action in spite of fear.

CAT Nip

Here are some things you can tell yourself when you are stuck:

- How fascinating!
- It's not the end of the world, for goodness sake!
- I will live another day to tell the story.
- Let's backtrack and see what went wrong.
- It could have been a lot worse!
- Hmm, what can I learn from this episode?
- Adversity builds character.
- Five years from now, how important will this seem?

A young employee of a firm made a mistake that cost the company a great deal of money.

The boss called him into the office, and he thought he was going to be fired. But the boss said, "Fire you! Not on your life. You have just had $10,000 worth of experience, and we have all learned from your mistake. Just don't let it happen again."

Ponder that.

A CAT'S Eye View of Life 7

Physicians have patient care audits and formal review committees. They know that mistakes are made in medicine, as much as we might hope that physicians are perfect. Their professional commitment is to learn from mistakes. Scientists keep lab notes, where a summary of what worked and what didn't work is added at the end. Perhaps you should record and analyze your failures as well, always saying to yourself, "What can I learn from this?"

LIFE 8

CATS Fail Early and Fail Well

We will all fail, but will we fail in a way that maximizes our chances to succeed?

Since you are going to have failures in any enterprise that includes risk, why not take advantage of this fact by loading the front end of the process with as much constructive failure as possible? This is what it means to fail well—for fail you will. The road to innovation is littered with failures. They will happen to us all. The real question is, "Do you want to take advantage of something that will happen regardless, or do you want pretend that you are the one exception to the rule and put you and your project at risk?"

Rapid Prototyping, IDEO Style

At IDEO headquarters in Palo Alto, there is a display containing artifacts of past projects. There you will find a five-gallon jar full of dozens of objects, all faintly resembling a computer mouse.

The jar is full of prototypes. Tom Kelley of IDEO put it this way, and I paraphrase: "You can put all your time and energy into finding the best possible result and present to your boss only to have her throw up all over it. [Kelley is quite illustrative.] Or you can quickly put together five or six prototypes and have a discussion with the boss [client] about her reaction to each of these concepts. And then take the ideas gained and create the next prototypes."

For me, this is the idea of failing early and failing well in order to have the best chance to succeed. Get feedback early, and get feedback that is rich in useful information. Failure is a part of the process whenever risk is involved. Don't resist it; embrace it for its information value. Minimize risk when you can, and you minimize risk when your failures come early in the process. This is the key to quick prototyping.

BusinessWeek carried an article about IDEO and how design firms were not only selling their design services but also were selling their understanding of innovation in the form of education and training for companies. In the article, the IDEO way of innovation was presented as five steps:

1. Observation—a number of methods to fully understand the customer experience
2. Brainstorming
3. Rapid prototyping
4. Refining
5. Implementation

Rapid prototyping is the step that incorporates failing well. IDEO has mastered this tool.

Learning from Cats

The maxim that cats always land on their feet has some truth to it. Curiosity at times puts cats in dangerous places like trees. But cats are endowed with survival skills that are often their salvation in these perilous situations. Most notable is their uncanny ability to spin in midair and land on all four paws.

Studies have shown that cats have a better chance of surviving a fall from a moderate height than a shorter drop. (What kind of person would conduct such research?) This is so because a shorter falling distance does not provide a sufficient buffer to execute their instinctive spin—much like not allowing enough time for a parachute to open before landing. There are records of cats falling 200 feet and surviving.

So what can falling cats teach us about failure? I have absolutely no idea, but isn't that interesting!

Rapid Prototyping in a Large Organization

I spent a highly educational 16 months working for the Veterans Administration (VA) in Washington, DC. My job at the VA was part of my education as a member of the fifth class of the President's Executive Exchange Program. This program, started by Lyndon Johnson and continued by successive presidents, had as its goal a better understanding between the private and government sectors. All the participants had jobs. The government participants went to GM, AT&T, IBM, and other large companies. Those of us in the private sector were assigned to the VA, the Department of Defense, the State Department, and the like. And there was an amazing educational program as well as a trip to Brussels to get a close view of the emerging European Community. The year was 1975.

Spending a year in the VA was the most intense education of my life. My assignment was to manage the VA evaluation team that visited hospitals and evaluated their compliance with VA and Joint Commission on Accreditation of Hospitals (JCAH) rules and regulations. There were 172 hospitals, so we stayed busy. I was a short-term employee and therefore nonthreatening. That gave me the latitude to mess around with interesting stuff. I decided to tackle a subject that is a ubiquitous potential problem in large bureaucratic organizations—communication.

The specific form of the problem at the VA was that the chief medical director (CMD) would craft a memo regarding a change that he would like to see in the organization. The change most often affected employees on or close to the front line. Great care would be taken to choose just the right words and phases; hence the memo had many authors as it was passed around for review. Then the memo would make its way through the layers and arrive at the bottom rung. The staff would read the directive, complete with interpretations from each level, and then would rush to implement the directive. There was usually a deadline that was reasonable at the time the memo was written, but because of the delays in passing information through the levels, there was always a time crunch at the bottom.

Staff would work around the clock and proudly pass their results back up the organization's ladder, only to find out after some delay that they had misinterpreted the assignment.

This happened often enough as to be extremely frustrating to the CMD. Having done some work on organizational development, I proposed that I study the problem as part of my duties, a suggestion that was approved immediately. I only studied the problem for a short time because I had seen similar problems often enough to know the cause. But I waited a reasonable amount of time before I went back to the CMD and proposed the following changes in protocol:

- Send the assignment directly to the level at which the problem would be addressed, and copy only those who needed to know.
- Meet with the team assigned to clarify the project.
- Suggest that the team divide its time into segments and spend the first segment coming up with at least three approaches to the solution.
- Meet with the CMD and present the alternatives, discuss, and make appropriate changes.
- Finish the project and deliver the results.

The middle levels of the organization were horrified at the prospect of being left out, and the rumor mill buzzed for weeks. However, it took only one trial for the CMD to see the value. The first team that came back with two prototypes of their approach had it half right but missed an important point. The CMD clarified his intentions in a two-way dialogue, and the team came back with an acceptable solution.

CAT Nip

Explain the VA story to a colleague, and discuss places in your work life that could benefit from a little prototyping.

The "Queasy Eagle" Award

In a *Harvard Business Review* article entitled, "Mapping Your Innovation Strategy," authors S. D. Anthony, M. Eyring, and L. Gibson, highlight three items under the heading "Changing the Innovation Mindset." Two of the three relate to failure. They are:

- Good enough can be great.
- The right kind of failure is success.

The authors cite an example from the Mayo Clinic, where the "Queasy Eagle" award is given to individuals who fail for the right reason. In response to this, I must say, "How fascinating!" The authors go on to remind us that "the initial strategy for a growth business is often going to be wrong." Managers need to recognize that learning what's wrong with an approach and adapting it appropriately is a "good failure." This sounds a lot like prototyping.

What do you think of the idea of having an award for those who fail well?

A CAT'S Eye View of Life 8

When you walk though the offices of IDEO in Palo Alto, you will see evidence of prototyping. IDEO does not believe in the myth of the lone genius. The process of innovation used at IDEO includes the creation of prototypes or models and lots of discussion. With physical products, the first prototypes are often made of Styrofoam and are crude to look at. Tom Kelley, former general manager of IDEO, told me that you have to learn how to "squint," an idea that has found a way into a great many of my discussions about innovation. I saw a jar full of computer mouses (I don't think *mice* works here), a product innovated by IDEO, and I asked why so many? The answer was that on the mouse project, the company wanted to be able to "see" the subtle differences.

The concept is simple: Build some prototypes quickly to stimulate discussions with the innovation team or with the client. Learn from those discussions, and repeat as needed.

Mick the Juggler also understands failing well. When you are trying to develop muscle memory, you want to be sure your focus is on the appropriate form rather than on "catching the ball." When your focus is on catching the ball and you reach here and reach there, you are teaching your body the wrong way to do it. Failing well is all about success in juggling.

LIFE 9

CAT Wranglers Understand Natural Energy

Cat Wranglers bring out the best in CATS. CATS thrive in an environment rich in natural energy.

CATS live in organizations, and those organizations all say that they value innovation.

But an organization is geared to operate, not innovate. It suffers from its own form of the norm and has trouble escaping. Of course, that norm actually resides in employees, but I said enough about that at the beginning of this book. We can take a few shortcuts now.

CAT Wranglers have the requisite skills to make sure the words of innovation are followed by the actions of innovation. They are a force for organizational integrity. The primary fuel for innovation is natural energy, and CAT Wranglers have a special understanding of personal energy.

Natural Energy

The best fuel for innovation is natural energy. Consider the opposite: toxic energy. It is hard to imagine a boss saying, "I want 20 percent more creativity from you incompetents or I'll shave your whiskers." Since innovation is voluntary and comes from the inside, it must be supported, fostered, and invited. It can't be demanded, forced, or coerced. CAT Wranglers understand this, and this understanding is the source of their special contribution to personal innovation inside any complex organization.

Human energy has always held a fascination for me. Early in my life, I marveled at how students who were labeled by teachers as "not motivated" would play basketball or baseball for hours after school.

In the corporate world, I experienced a similar phenomenon. I observed that employees often were labeled as deadbeats and written off as someone simply interested in earning a paycheck with no real commitment to the organization. These same employees, when given a few degrees of freedom and an invitation to engage, often would come alive. The energy and vitality were there just under the surface, but it took someone with the skills of a CAT Wrangler to collaborate on their release.

"What has come over John?" colleagues would ask.

It is natural energy.

"How is it that Mary raised so much money for leukemia research when she is such a blob at work?"

It is natural energy.

Top street performers can help us understand the power of this energy. They are one-person businesses that make a living from volunteers. No one is forced to form a circle around a street performer. No one is forced to stay for the performance, and many don't. No one is forced to put money in the hat when it is passed at the end of the performance. And street performers know that the amount of money in the hat will be correlated with the amount of natural energy that was present.

This relationship is a universal law of humanity. It is the same for clerks, tellers, sales people, accountants, attorneys, doctors, teachers, and managers. In each of these professions, there are skills to be mastered, but the biggest hat pass, whether it be real-time feedback, performance reviews, customer surveys, or bonuses, is usually an indicator of the amount of natural energy that was present over the performance period. The authentic, vulnerable, and fully human connections are unsurpassed in their energy-releasing power.

CATS thrive on natural energy, and CAT Wranglers must be specialists in it.

Natural Energy Review

- ***Natural energy*** **is another name for** ***authentic energy*****. It is energy that flows from choice and commitment rather than obligation or fear.**
- **Natural energy is the energy of freedom, not the energy of oppression. Freedom, in this context, is in part the freedom to be yourself.**
- **Natural energy can't be demanded, coerced, or manipulated. It can only be invited, inspired, discovered, and modeled. CAT Wranglers understand this.**

- **Natural energy is not a result of being strategic but an outcome of being human.**
- ***Shallow*, *forced*, *toxic*, *inauthentic*, *unpleasant*, *phony*, and *arrogant* are words we use when the energy isn't natural.**
- **A high quality of work life, a rich customer experience, and real motivation and innovation are enhanced by an environment rich in natural energy.**

CAT Wranglers and FISH®

I devoted the 10 years prior to the publication of this book to traveling the world and speaking about the ideas in my book, *FISH!*. Although I wrote the book, most of what I know about the ideas in it I learned from people like you who discovered their own way to bring the FISH! philosophy to life in the workplace, each example an innovation.

I never cease to be amazed by the novel examples of FISH! in action. And I observed that all the places where FISH! was alive and vital were full of natural energy. In fact, this was the provocation to coin the term *natural energy*.

The leaders I found in these organizations were special. In one of the early editions of *Fast Company*, Morris Masterson—then CEO of Perot Systems—wrote an article entitled, "Everything I Knew about Leadership Was Wrong." That was exactly how I felt only a few years into my journey. Everything I thought I knew about leadership was wrong or incomplete. I began to think of leadership as having three distinct faces.

Three Faces of Leadership

Each of the faces of leadership described below has a place and a time. Two of the faces are familiar to any student of business or any manager. But only one of the faces maximizes the natural energy needed for innovation, and it is *not* well known, that is, except for CAT Wranglers.

The *first face of leadership* focuses on directing and controlling. It is an efficient form of leadership and is described using such words as *control, alignment, incentives, overcoming resistance, team play,* and *winning one for the "gipper."* It can be kind, but it is one-directional. The leader tells the followers what to do and uses a variety of tools to ensure that they do what they are told. The result is *compliance.*

The *second face of leadership* focuses on participation. It takes more time up front than the first face because it requires interaction with followers. Such words as *feedback, push back, involvement,* and *buy-in* are used frequently. The leader lets the followers have a say in a decision and then announces the course of action. The result of this form of leadership is *cooperation.*

The *third face of leadership* focuses on invitation. Followers are treated like volunteers and choose their degree of involvement. Such words as *trust, authenticity, inspiration,* and *vulnerability* are common. The leader invites the followers to engage in a conversation about what is being created together with life energy. The leader models that which she is hoping to inspire in the followers. The result of this form of leadership is *collaboration* and *commitment*. This is the home of the CAT Wrangler, who knows that innovation is voluntary and that natural energy is the fuel.

3M Has a Long History of CAT Wrangling

I have lived in the city that boasts the corporate headquarters of 3M—St. Paul, Minnesota—for most of my life and have 3M employees as friends and acquaintances. Because the headquarters employs so many, the town is aware of and interested in the well-being of 3M. Yes, there is also great interest in Cargill, Medtronic, Target, and United Health Group—all headquartered in Minnesota. But I am especially interested in 3M because it has taken on legendary status for innovation. 3M is a company the world of business respects for its innovation.

In 1948, its founder, William M. McKnight, outlined core values that, not surprisingly, are similar to the values highlighted in this book. McKnight is a great example of a CAT Wrangler.

William M. McKnight Quote (1948)

As our business grows, it becomes increasingly necessary to delegate responsibility and to encourage men and women to exercise their initiative. This requires considerable tolerance. Those men and women, to whom we delegate authority and

responsibility, if they are good people, are going to want to do their jobs in their own way.

Mistakes will be made. But if a person is essentially right, the mistakes he or she makes are not as serious in the long run as the mistakes management will make if it undertakes to tell those in authority exactly how they must do their jobs.

Management that is destructively critical when mistakes are made kills initiative. And it's essential that we have many people with initiative if we are to continue to grow.

3M is also known for its *15 percent rule*, where employees are given time to pursue innovative ideas outside their primary work assignment. I was conducting a seminar at 3M, and during the break, I was talking informally with some of the participants. Three guys were off by themselves, and I walked over and asked where they worked, assuming they worked together. They identified three different parts of 3M. I asked if they had known each other before this seminar. 3M is a big place, and they proceeded to tell me that they were working on "a 15 percent project." Together they had developed and were launching a special kind of product used to contain oil spills. Now *that* is a leadership environment that respects natural energy.

Invisible CAT Wrangling

Sometimes it is possible to build a system or structure that promotes what CAT Wranglers would otherwise need to do. At Sharp Electronics, the company had a problem. The staff of the most critical new projects had difficulty getting the attention of those from whom they needed help. All projects were pretty much treated the same at Sharp, so when a member of the team working on a high-leverage, future-of-the-company project approached someone for help, he was placed in the cue behind all the other demands on that person.

The solution was a symbol worn by the members of high-leverage teams. A large gold star was given to every member of the team, and the word went out that whenever a person with a gold star asks for your help, you drop what you are doing and provide that help. Problem solved with indirect leadership.

The CAT Wrangler Manifesto

If you decide you want to be a CAT Wrangler, here is a place to start. Read "The CAT Wrangler Manifesto," and look for things you can do to become a better CAT Wrangler.

- CAT Wranglers provide a clear and consistent vision of work and of the way people will work together.
- CAT Wranglers know that innovation is best fueled with natural energy.
- CAT Wranglers know that natural energy is free, abundant, and waiting to be released inside every CAT.

- CAT Wranglers encourage a variety of ideas, including those that make them uncomfortable.
- CAT Wranglers welcome creative conflict and work to make sure that creative conflict doesn't turn into personal conflict.
- CAT Wranglers seek out the weird, wacky, unconventional, and deviant. They are not happy if things get too comfortable, and they don't want everyone to fit in.
- CAT Wranglers see their job as serving CATS by removing obstacles, providing resources, and running interference when the rest of the organization tries to expel the "misfit creatives."
- CAT Wranglers find opportunity in unlikely places because they look for it.
- CAT Wranglers are nice to their mothers.
- CAT Wranglers are effective as arbitrators of disputes between innovators because they have earned the trust of their associates.
- CAT Wranglers walk the talk by making frequent personal use of the Nine Lives of Innovation.
- CAT Wranglers understand the role of failure in innovation.
- CAT Wranglers understand that there is a place for freedom within certain boundaries

and that those boundaries are much wider than most leaders think.

- CAT Wranglers know that CATS thrive on a sense of spaciousness in their work environment.
- CAT Wranglers understand and practice the philosophy of Herb Kelleher, former chairman of Southwest Airlines, who said, "If you are leaning toward the customer, rather than away from the customer, we will forgive you anything you do."
- CAT Wranglers help other CATS flourish by giving them the freedom to be themselves. Herb Kelleher was once asked at a meeting of analysts, "But how do you keep control?" His reply? "Never had control. Don't want control." Yet Southwest is known for its innovation in service and was named one of America's most admired companies by *Fortune* magazine.
- CAT Wranglers understand and apply the language of energy.
- CAT Wranglers understand that the arrangement of people in an office and the design of traffic flows can promote provocation.
- CAT Wranglers design systems that do their work for them.

A CAT'S Eye View of Life 9

There is no better example of what natural energy looks like than the market that was the core of the book *FISH!*. At Pike Place Fish, the energy has been flowing naturally for two decades, and office workers come down to the market at lunch time just to hang out.

Much of the innovation at the market is innovation at the point of contact. The novelty is born from the customer interaction. You might observe the following scene at different times, but each is born out of the connection between customer and fishmonger:

"How are you going to pay for your fish?"

"With a credit card."

Customer gives credit card to fishmonger who returns after a long pause at the credit card machine and says, "Do you have another card?"

After a few moments of mild embarrassment, as the customer looks for another card or some cash, the fishmonger says, "I don't really need another card. I was just curious about whether you had one."

The principles of leadership that operate at the market will be found in any setting with natural energy. *Authentic, committed, respectful, tolerant, clear in vision,* and *egoless in action* all would be words that fit. When it comes to natural energy, Pike Place Fish is it. That's what it looks like.

PART TWO

Sustaining a CAT'S Life

Sustaining a CAT'S life can be difficult and challenging. There is always the gravity pull of old ways of doing things. A CAT needs a special diet of renewal with occasional supplements of inspiration and, of course, provocation. It is also helpful to have a little CAT Nip that you can pull out of the bottom drawer when you need it or perhaps an occasional challenge that will stretch you and keep you focused. But no matter what the situation, always remember . . . .

Always Remember

- **Remember, you are capable of innovating. This capability comes with your membership in the human race.**
- **Remember, you don't have to be bad at innovation to get better.**
- **Remember, you are capable of learning, understanding, and putting into practice any one or all of the tools and concepts presented in *CATS: The Nine Lives of Innovation*.**
- **Remember, bringing innovation to the world and using your unique gifts to benefit others are what gives life meaning.**
- **Remember, you are now ready and able.**

The only remaining consideration is

Are you willing?

There are two things you can start doing immediately to make the material in *CATS* a bigger part of your life. You can Mind Map the content and regularly review and embellish your map. And you can teach other prospective CATS the highlights of what you learned.

CHAPTER 5

A Personal Review of the Nine Lives

One of the best ways to live a long and productive life as a CAT is to regularly review the Nine Lives of Innovation. To help you with this review and assessment, I have prepared a series of questions to contemplate. This is not a section to be read in one sitting. It is a section to be sampled a little at a time, each time thinking, "How can I act on this in my own life?"

Before you begin the review and assessment, you should prepare. Start by making a personal commitment to fully engage in the process. Remember that this is a learning event and that, on occasion, you will be stumped. At those times, you might be heard to say, "How fascinating! What can I learn from this?"

Review of the Four Basic Challenges to Innovation

The Challenge of Clutter, Doubts, Fears, Voices, and Toxic Workplaces

The doubts and fears accumulated over a lifetime are there, in part, to keep us safe and secure. They also can serve as a straightjacket, preventing innovation. The noise created by the clutter of life can drown out thoughts and remove all the spaciousness so important to innovation.

- Have you listened to the voices?
- Are you aware of the amount of clutter in your life?
- Have you found ways to reduce the clutter?
- Can you make your workplace a more lighthearted environment?
- Have you looked at your life and sorted it into two categories—life that needs spaciousness and life that works just fine amid the clutter and distraction?
- Will you create more spaciousness when you need it?

The Challenge of Being Normal

In order to survive as human beings, we are endowed with the ability to develop routines, patterns, and standard approaches to many of life's tasks. In fact, normal is the default position of the brain. Innovation requires getting outside the norms, and this is no small task given the amount of practice we have simply being normal. Hence a major challenge to innovation is our normality.

- Can you name your dominant paradigms for personal relationships?
- Can you name the routines you follow when at work?
- Do you have a favorite way of chilling out after work?
- Do you hear yourself saying things your mother and father said?
- Can you see the many ways you are normal?

The Challenge of Failure

Even though failure is fundamental to learning, most of us grow up trying to avoid failure. We are punished for making mistakes. Our school grades are directly correlated with the number of mistakes we make. Our coaches remove us from the game if we make mistakes. Who wakes up in the morning saying, "I think I will devote this day to failure"? To make progress, we must come to grips with the importance of failure in learning and innovation. To innovate, we must understand and at times even embrace failure.

- Had any failures today?
- Yesterday?
- Had a big one lately?

- Had the same one twice?
- Can you name something good that came out of a recent setback?
- What is your view of others who have failures?
- How do you view failure as a manager or an employee?
- Have you ever failed in a really embarrassing way?

The Challenge of Leadership

All innovation is change, and any change brings challenges. Our willingness to try new things, especially in an organizational context, is in part a function of the climate established by leaders. But the old leadership styles are not capable of creating a safe haven for innovation; a different approach is necessary.

Innovation is primarily a voluntary activity that comes from the inside; hence leadership techniques that focus on the outside are not appropriate. Leadership grounded in concepts derived from a strategic mindset is not big enough to embrace the human spirit of a CAT. Concepts such as alignment, core competence, direction, control, monitoring, quality assurance, statistical process control, measurement, incentives, and strategic intent are not helpful at the personal level. Working with CATS requires a different kind of leadership, one not often taught in business schools. This is the challenge of leadership.

- Have you ever worked on a hot team that was really challenged and where the energy was high and creative sparks were always flying?
- Have you ever worked for or observed a maternal or paternal leader in a nonadult-adult relationship with a direct report?
- Are there times when followers encourage the point of view that they depend on leaders to take care of them?
- Have you observed the nature of leadership in a highly creative environment such as IDEO?
- Do you have a clear sense of how you are best led for innovation?

Review of The Nine Lives of Innovation

Life 1: CATS Create an Innovation Friendly Environment

The first life of innovation is about quieting the noise, acting in the face of fear, setting aside the voices of judgment, and creating a playful environment that overwhelms the negatives that are always in the wings waiting for a chance to take root.

- Have you developed a practice of setting aside time, away from the clutter, to think and to dream?
- Are you fully aware of the numbing effect of busyness for the sake of being busy?

- Have you learned to listen to the voices of judgment inside your head and in the world as a curious observer?
- Have you generated your own clutter by passing time attending meetings, moving paper around the desk, and surfing the Internet with no real purpose?
- How often do you look down at your personal digital assistant (PDA)?
- Are you aware that looking at your PDA takes you away from the present?
- Are you aware that innovation happens in the present?
- Can you learn to set aside special times to look at your e-mail?
- Can you see personal implications for the idea that courage is not the absence of fear but rather acting in the face of fear?

Life 2: CATS Are Always Prepared

Being prepared for innovation is an often-overlooked step. Because innovation happens in the moment, it is necessary to be prepared for that moment. This means having immediate access to your mental filing cabinets. This immediate and random access allows you to bring things to the mix in an instant when the creative sparks are flying. Being prepared also means having some understanding of the content. It would be hard, but not impossible, to innovate in a field where you had no understanding of the basic content. Depending on the nature of the innovation sought, content can extend over a wide range of knowledge. Observing how people interact, experiencing a culture, studying history, learning the laws of optics, reading biographies, learning about nanotechnology, and studying the evolution of a honey bee are all possible ways to prepare.

- Are you committed to learning?
- Do you think about how you are storing your knowledge?
- Have you prepared a radiant map, like a Mind Map®, of each key area of content that you want to have available in the moment?
- Can you think of ways to meet new people and widen your social and professional network?
- Have you considered a new hobby?
- Is there a content area that you used to love but have not visited recently?
- Have you read anything new lately?
- Can you remember that the key is to enrich your life with new experiences, new contacts, and new knowledge so that you build a repository from which to draw when the muse appears?
- Do you claim your pitch?
- Is your attitude a part of your claim?

Life 3: CATS Know that Innovation Isn't Normal

This may be the most important life. I say this because if you don't understand the power of the norm and the role of associative boundaries, the tools you need to embrace on the road to innovation will seem frivolous and Bohemian. Perhaps the biggest mistake made by that wonderful cohort of people who call themselves creativity or innovation consultants is that they don't take the time to show people why the techniques they teach are necessary. It is the fact that people live in the norm that keeps them from seeing the norm from a different perspective.

- Take a current project and ask yourself, "If I was willing to defy all norms and really stretch the envelope, what would I do differently?"
- Do you understand the relationship between associative boundaries and the fact that you are normal?
- Can you make a practice of stretching your associative boundaries by arbitrarily choosing to do things you always do one way in a different way?
- Can you make a game of it? (How many routes can I take to work? If I had to do this task in a radically different way, how could I approach it?)
- Can you take a routine activity and make it more fun by changing your approach?

- Can you think of other ways to increase the novelty in your life?

Life 4: CATS Welcome Physical Provocation

Physical provocation is one of three types of provocation that can help you to escape the routine in order to have an opportunity to see the innovative. This form of provocation can come from the use of space, design of surroundings, objects, a break, or a daydream.

- Do you bring objects into meetings to provoke ideas?
- Have you tried to take a break as a way to get the work done?
- Were you able to completely escape and give your subconscious a chance to talk to you?
- What did your subconscious have to say?
- Do you keep a record of the results of your breaks?
- Have you considered rearranging your workspace for the purpose of provocation?
- Do you have a special place to think?
- Are you aware of what energizes you?
- Have you considered emersion in another culture, geography, or job for its provocation value and novelty?
- Are you finding novel ways to stimulate the Medici Effect?

- Do the leaders in your organization regularly spend time doing the jobs on the front line?
- Are the workers on the front line invited to experience the executive suite?

Life 5: CATS Enjoy Social Provocation

Social provocation is the provocation that comes from interacting with other people and encountering their thoughts and emotions. Brainstorming is the dominant form of social provocation discussed in the literature, but there is a more common form that is so natural as to be missed completely. That is the provocation happening at the point of contact between two people. This, in fact, is the primary source of innovation in the world, and it is especially critical in the service industry, where the brand and repeat business depend in part on innovation at the point of contact. Practicing innovation at the point of contact by making novel, authentic, and personal connections brings into play many of the Nine Lives of Innovation. Getting better at innovation at the point of contact should improve your capacity to innovate anywhere because it requires reducing the power of the associative boundaries.

- Do you have a set of guidelines for brainstorming?
- Have you considered the hazards of brainstorming?
- Do you have a personal referent for innovation at the point of contact?

- Can you observe yourself bringing novelty, authenticity, and integrity to your personal engagements?
- Have you felt resistance to the vulnerability that accompanies real encounters?
- Have you ever bounced off the ideas of another person and developed a new insight?
- Can you use words and ideas for their movement value?
- Do you work harder with a personal trainer?

Life 6: CATS Promote Intellectual Provocation

Intellectual provocation is invisible unless you choose to make it external because it all happens in your head. When you play games with your mind by considering the opposite, using random words, assaulting your thinking with the impossible, and changing the rules, you are engaging in intellectual provocation. While not the most efficient of the provocations, it is like the reverse gear in your car. It may not get used very often, but when you need it, you need it.

- Have you developed a comfort level with intellectual provocation?
- Have you tried the random-word technique?
- Do you understand the reason lateral thinking works?
- Have you thought about jokes and why they are funny?

- Can you see the reason for random-word techniques?
- Have you practiced playing with ideas?
- Can you use an idea for its movement value?

Life 7: CATS Say "How Fascinating!"

Making mistakes is an important part of life, yet most of us grow up with a fear of failure that we must overcome to innovate. This fear of failure has many sources, including well-meaning parents and teachers who want us to succeed in life but have a limited view of success. The truth is that any significant advancement requires a whole lot of failure, and while you may not want to fail repeatedly at something important to you or the organization, you must learn the importance of failure in learning in order to put it in perspective.

- Do you keep a journal of your flubs?
- Do you make a practice of saying, "How Fascinating! What can I learn from this?"
- Have you considered sponsoring an award at work for the most magnificent screw-up?
- Have you considered competing for that award?
- Have you found ways to embrace and enjoy mistakes for the important contribution they make to your learning?
- Have you celebrated a great mistake lately?

Life 8: CATS Fail Early and Fail Well

Failure is not an option—it will happen any time there is risk—and innovation is a risky business. This life suggests that you organize your failures for maximum learning and that you get your failures out of the way early rather than having one big one at the end of a project.

- Do you look for ways to use rapid prototyping?
- Can you identify places in your life where failing early and learning from the mistakes could have saved you time or money or anguish?
- Can you see how the following statement is connected to failing early and well? "What we need to do in this change effort is to teach those who are targeted to change how to resist that change effectively."
- Can you see how having the right people talking to each other at the beginning of a project might avoid the common bureaucratic result of having a solution or result that does not match the intention or vision?
- When you are assigned a project do you immediately think of ways to prototype it?

Life 9: CAT Wranglers Understand Natural Energy

All innovation is change, and innovation that occurs in the context of a complex organization requires the help of a special kind of leader. These Leader CATS, or CAT Wranglers as I love to call them, are critical to the successful development and implementation of an innovation.

- Have you considered seeking out someone you respect as a CAT Wrangler and asking her if she would be your mentor?
- Do you have a clear understanding of natural energy?
- Do you see the humor in the statement, "I want 30 percent more creativity out of you tomorrow or you are fired?"
- Have you considered meeting with the people you supervise and asking for feedback on your leadership practices?
- Do you make leadership a hobby and accumulate the best ideas in a journal?
- Have you observed the kind of leadership practices that don't work in your organization's quest to innovate?
- Do you see the connection between a FISH! environment and CATS?

CHAPTER 6

Earning a CAT Belt in Innovation

In this chapter you will find a description of three CAT Belts you can earn by completing some specific assignments. Do the work and earn the corresponding CAT Belt.

These tasks are meant to be done thoughtfully, so try to spread them over a number of days. Don't rush it. Use the pursuit of a CAT Belt as an excuse to have some fun! Get a partner, and work together. Get someone in the family involved. Find energy where you can.

I recommend that you undertake the belts in order. Good luck, and keep in touch:

www.catsinnovation.com

www.topperformer.com

The First-Degree CAT Belt

In 1970, I decided to be a writer. I had coauthored a technical book in my late twenties. That book probably sold a couple dozen copies, and even though my role was small, I enjoyed the process.

In 1980, I had yet to write another book. Not an atypical career in writing—a lot of dreaming and planning but no action. It was about that time that I came in contact with Stephen Covey and his ideas. I decided to accept the challenge of seeing if the words and deeds of my life were in harmony. One of the roles I identified in this process was *writer*.

After a few more years, *writer* was still on the list of roles, but no books had even been started. I did an integrity check and noted the obvious: The role *writer* lacked integrity because I wasn't writing. My words and deeds were not in alignment with writer. So I challenged myself saying, "Self, either you start writing or the role *writer* will be removed from your list." That was all it took. I became a real writer. I wrote for myself. I wrote for my students. I wrote articles. I wrote nonsense in my journal, but I wrote. This is what writers do and what make them writers—they write.

This story is a common story. It is a story about what Steven Pressfield calls "resistance." It is an important subject for CATS. To earn the first-degree CAT Belt, you must explore your resistance.

This first-degree CAT Belt is canary yellow. There is a reason. Miners used to carry birdcages into the mines. In each cage was a canary. When the canary flopped over on its back, the miner knew the air was foul. The first-degree CAT Belt is about keeping your canary alive.

Assignment

Monitor your resistance to the things you have been putting off in your life. You know what they are! At the end of two weeks, establish your goals for something you really want to do but have been resisting. In his powerful little book, Steven Pressfield calls *resistance* the biggest hurdle faced by anyone who wishes to make a difference in the world. If you have time, find Pressfield's book and read it. This is not required reading for the CAT Belt (the book is hard to find), but it would be well worth the effort.

Resource

Steven Pressfield, *The War of Art: Break Through the Blocks and Win Your Inner Creative Battles*. New York: First Warner Books, 2003.

The Second-Degree CAT Belt

The second-degree CAT Belt is green, reminding us of the verdant nature of innovation. To earn this belt of green, *do one* of the following assignments:

1. Engage in strenuous physical exercise, exercise that will put you in the "zone" at a time when you can't seem to come up with an idea you need to complete a project, chapter, paper, talk, workshop, or other engagement. Record any

useful ideas that came into your consciousness while exercising.

2. Apply the concept of quick prototyping to a work project.

3. Consciously use the words of others for their movement value in a brainstorming session; bounce off word provocations to find yourself in new and unexplored territory.

4. Read one of Edward de Bono's books on lateral thinking. Describe lateral thinking to a friend.

5. Make a suggestion for how the book *CATS* might be improved, and e-mail the author at slrunner@aol.com.

When you have completed your green-belt assignment, you are only one step from Whiskers. Celebrate for a moment, and then go to www.catsinnovation.com and look at the distinguished List of Whiskers on which your name will soon be placed. I'd love to hear from you as well.

Resources

Edward de Bono, *Lateral Thinking*. New York: Harper Paperbacks, 1973.

Edward de Bono, *Po: Beyond Yes and No*. International Center for Creative Thinking, 1990.

Edward de Bono, *I Am Right: You Are Wrong*. New York: Penguin Books, 1992.

Third-Degree CAT Belt

The third-degree CAT Belt signifies that you are ready to teach others in the ways of the CAT. If you are willing to accept this challenge, please continue. The belt worn by those called *Whiskers* is a black belt, to reflect the precious nature of what you have to offer.

It is said that if you want to learn something really well, teach someone else. To earn the black belt, you need to *do any one* of the following:

- Attend a CATS Certification Course.
- Make a presentation about CATS at work.
- Teach CATS to your children.
- Conduct a seminar on CATS.

Once you achieve the black CAT Belt, you can be called *Whiskers*.

Visit www.catsinnovation.com and register your achievement so that we can celebrate your milestone and invite you to join the CATS Community.

Visit www.topperformer.com to have more fun.

Let me know if you want to become a part of the Whiskers Training Team.

CHAPTER 7

CATS as a Taxonomy for Personal Innovation Tools and Concepts

As I was field testing *CATS: The Nine Lives of Innovation*, I was surprised by how often people commented about the organizing capability of CATS. While creating CATS, I had as a goal being able to organize the universe of personal development tools, tools such as Mind Mapping® and Six Hats®. I didn't expect the reader or workshop attendee to have that as a goal. I guess it is further testimony to how confusing the plethora of tools and concepts for creativity and innovation might be for some.

One of the reasons for this confusion is the natural tendency of those who develop tools—people like me—to try and make the tool we created fit a vast array of circumstances.

"Having problems with your marriage? Try FISH!®"

"Constipated? Try FISH!"

"Money problems? FISH! will help."

Multiply this by dozens of tools, hundreds of concepts, and tens of thousands of workshops and you can see how it could get muddled in the mind of any individual. Since this book is for individuals, it made sense to do something about that mess.

Below I have matched tools, techniques, and people with lives. In so doing, I am identifying what I consider the most likely uses, knowing full well that my colleagues may have a different opinion. I mean no offense; it is simply my take.

I know I will make mistakes. My Web site will present changes, additions, and apologies. If you find a mistake or missing tool, let me know so that I can say, "How Fascinating!" This is a beginning, not the last word.

Please note that when a tool or concept is listed, I believe that tool or concept is a good fit for the life under which it is listed. Where you see only a name, I am simply giving credit to a person or organization that has made a major contribution to my understanding or my use of that life. There are also combinations where both are true.

Life 1: CATS Create an Innovation Friendly Environment

- Meditation
- FISH!

- Stanford MBA course in creativity
- Compression Planning—Jerry McNellis

Life 2: CATS Are Prepared

- Mind Mapping—Tony Buzan
- Claim Your Pitch®—Carr Hagerman
- *Top Performer®* video

Life 3: CATS Know that Innovation Isn't Normal

- Paradigms
- Associative boundaries
- Thomas Kuhn
- Joel Barker
- Gordon MacKenzie and the "Giant Hairball"

Life 4: CATS Welcome Physical Provocation

- *The Medici Effect*—Frans Johansson
- IDEO—tech box
- An idea collection

Life 5: CATS Enjoy Social Provocation

- Brainstormer—IDEO
- Brainstorming—Alex Osborne
- Compression planning—Jerry McNellis

- *Six Thinking Hats*—Edward de Bono
- Juice the Jam®—*Top Performer* video and book

Life 6: CATS Promote Intellectual Provocation

- *Lateral Thinking*—Edward de Bono
- *PO*—Edward de Bono
- *A Whack in the Side of the Head*—Roger von Oech

Life 7: CATS Say "How Fascinating!"

- Tony Buzan
- *Mick the Juggler* (Ontend® video)
- The learning curve

Life 8: CATS Fail Early and Fail Well

- IDEO
- Ready, fire, aim

Life 9: CAT Wranglers Understand Natural Energy

- Natural Energy®—Carr Hagerman
- *Top Performer* video and book (Ontend Creative Partners)
- *The Three Faces of Leadership*—Stephen Lundin
- *FISH!* and *FISH! Sticks*—Stephen Lundin, Harry Paul, and John Christensen

CHAPTER 8

More Stuff

In the field of innovation, there are many talented people and a few certified geniuses, like Edward de Bono, Tony Buzan, and David Whyte, all of whom have dedicated their life to creativity and innovation in their own way. De Bono brought us lateral thinking and a host of creative tools, whereas Buzan has provided Mind Mapping®. And Whyte explores the essence of innovation in everyday life through his poetry and prose.

Joining these three innovators extraordinaire are thousands of writers, artists, teachers, consultants, and others who have a useful perspective, a thoughtful framework, or a tool heralded as something you need in order for you or your organization to innovate.

A few resources are listed below. My goal has not been to present an exhaustive list but simply to identify a few of my favorites. Many of these are mentioned elsewhere in this book.

- *The Art of Innovation* by Tom Kelley
- *Orbiting the Giant Hairball* by Gordon MacKenzie
- *The Innovator's Dilemma* and *The Innovator's Solution* by Clayton Christensen
- *Brain Child* by Tony Buzan
- *Innovation to the Core* by Peter Skarzynski and Rowan Gibson
- *The Medici Effect* by Frans Johansson
- Anything written by David Whyte
- Anything written by Edward de Bono
- *Trust the Process* by Shaun McNiff

CHAPTER 9

The Bio of Whiskers One

Stephen C. Lundin

A.k.a. the Big Tuna Ph.D. and coauthor of the multimillion best-selling *FISH!*® books and coauthor of *Top Performer*®. Steve has been a working creative and a student of innovation and creativity for over 40 years. He is based in the United States. Over the last decade, Steve has taken his message to all parts of the globe, including multiple visits to Japan, India, Malaysia, Singapore, Mexico, Canada, Australia, New Zealand, Turkey, South Africa, much of Europe, and the United Arab Emirates.

He is a writer, speaker, filmmaker, one-time business school dean, serial entrepreneur, long-time adjunct member of MBA faculties, and former director of the Institute for Innovation and Creativity at the University of St. Thomas. He is also a cofounder of Ontend Creative Partners, the home of Top Performer and CATS.

Steve studied with Tony Buzan—originator of Mind Mapping®—stalked Dr. Edward de Bono—the man who conceptualized lateral thinking—whenever he traveled in North America, and studied IDEO—one of the world's most innovative organizations. He also immersed himself in the prose and poetry of creative genius and workplace visionary David Whyte.

Steve has had a lifelong dream of creating a framework for innovation that would make innovation more accessible to everyday people like him. In the last 10 years, a few key influences have helped him frame CATS. These influences include writing the *FISH!* series of books, observing that the FISH! philosophy is present in the most innovative organizations, and visiting IDEO. But the biggest influence of all was the tragic end to his long-distance running.

Steve has been an unskilled but passionate athlete who lettered in football, hockey, and track at Hamline University. Later he became involved with a group of misfits that ran races called *ultramarathons*. These were 50- and 100-mile races, often run on mountain trails. For about 15 years, Steve spent his morning hours and weekends covering insane distances on foot. Finding that he frequently ended a 50-mile run going downhill backwards because of knee pain, he eventually had his knee rebuilt. His running days were over, and he was depressed for months. Then something amazing happened. He began filling the sacred morning hours with writing. Without the knee injury, there would be no *CATS*.

Steve has taken his message to Microsoft, Standard Chartered Bank, Johnson & Johnson, 3M, Consolidated Banks of Africa, GlaxoSmithKline, Procter & Gamble, PriceWaterhouseCoopers, the Australian Institute of Management, the Singapore Institute of Management, the Knowledge Gym in New Zealand, and hundreds of other organizations around the world.

You can drop him a personal note at slrunner@aol.com. Be sure to join the CATS Community by going to www.catsinnovation.com.

A Final Thought

I am amazed at how many people are convinced they aren't creative and have no capacity to innovate. "I don't have a creative bone in my body," they admit as they watch someone fashioning the Taj Mahal out of seaweed. "I'm too conservative to be innovative," they offer as their spouse creates a five line poem out of snow flakes. The truth can be frightening. We all have the capacity to innovate and we all enjoy the wonderful feeling of having made a unique contribution. There may be individual differences in our associative boundaries and our comfort level with being weird, but that in no way limits our ability to make an innovative contribution. There is hope for all of us!

A few months ago I suggested my talented colleague, Gordon Boudreau, fashion a poem about being normal. It turned out to not only be brilliant, but in a whimsical way, it is a poem of hope. I hope his poem leaves you with a smile on your face and the confidence you need to develop your capacity to innovate in all aspects of your life.

STEPHEN C. LUNDIN, PH.D.
CHAIRMAN, ONTEND CREATIVE PARTNERS

Ode to Normal

By Gordon Boudreau
(Included with his permission.)

He was born on a day without portent or storm.
At the hour when they say that most babies are born.
Just an average day, neither hot nor too cold.
In a house rather like many others, I'm told.

And when he arrived the good doctor did state,
"Why, this baby has typical baby-like traits!
His size and his shape are wholly consistent
With data I've gathered from other such infants.

His head's nice and round, but not overly so.
A too-rotund head is not normal, you know!
His nose fits the bill, neither beakish nor squished-in.
And it sits in a place that's in tune with tradition."

His mother rejoiced at such welcoming news.
She kissed his fat cheeks till they nearly turned blue.
"Thank goodness! He's normal! Quite normal, I say!
He's normal in every appreciable way!"

Thus uttered, those words wove a palpable spell.
And normal became him, and served him quite well.
It gave him safe passage. It gave him good health.
And it kept him from making a fool of himself.

In school he played sports, and he dabbled in chess.
But mostly he tried to blend in with the rest.
If you look in the yearbook, a picture you'll see
Of him with his class in 1983.

That's him in the middle. Third row, seventh in.
With his hair parted just as they did way back then.
What's that? You can't find him? I'll point to the spot.
It's easy to miss him. He gets that a lot.

He passed through his schooling, respectably so.
His grades above average, but slightly, you know?
He found a good job, he found a good wife.
And settled on in to his linear life.

He adheres to the script. He follows the form.
He never does anything outside the norm.
In fact, that's his nickname. He's heard it before.
His friends yell "The Norm" when he walks through the door.

One day something happened that alters this poem.
The train had broke down, and he had to walk home.
As he walked through the park, he felt so fatigued
That he lay himself down and he fell fast asleep.

As it happens, a circus had come to that town.
And they formed a parade as he lay on the ground.
He awoke to a vision of jugglers and clowns.
From the ground it appeared that they walked upside down.

Upside-down camels, upside-down monkeys,
Upside-down strong men, gypsies and donkeys.
He might have sat up and corrected his view.
But for once he didn't do what he'd normally do.

He just lay on his back and looked up at this scene,
Till it faded away like a fanciful dream.
The vision receded. He lay there alone.
By and by he arose, but he didn't go home.

No. He tilted his head ten degrees to the right.
And he walked all around through the now-fading
light.
Down by the gardens. Out near the lake.
Through a graveyard with leaves piled next to a rake.

He didn't say a word. He didn't make a sound.
Till at length he stopped walking and sat himself
down.
And he wondered aloud at all that he'd seen,
And what lies in the space between normal and dreams.

What shall we call it? Perhaps openness?
A place of discovery, ideas, and risks.
To go from what's safe to those vast, unknown places,
And gather what treasures you find in the spaces.

For when you return, to step back through those doors,
Your normal will be where you left it before.
But newly informed by what walks upside down
In that curious land with the outlandish clowns.

But back to our hero. For later that night
He dined on the roof neath the stars, with his wife.
Sometimes they shoot pool with Wiffle ball bats.
They go to the opera in pinwheel hats.

And at work, he's the one that they turn to whenever
Their thinking is stuck and they need something clever.
He thinks for a while, and his eyes start to shimmer,
And he dares to give voice to what might be a winner.

His boss claps his shoulders and says with a grin,
"Great Scott, my good man, seems you've done it again."
And his friends gather round and they ask how such
thinking
Just springs from his mind. Is it luck? Is it ginseng?

He never explains it, but once in a while,
He'll cock his head sideways and give a sly smile.

People with whom I would like to share these ideas:

1.

2.

3.

4.

5.

Return this book to:

To find out more about CATS, CATS products, and the CATS Community, go to www.catsinnovation.com, or call our toll free number 888-544-9164.

If you wish, you can e-mail me directly at slrunner@aol.com.

Ontend Creative Partners
Box 497
Excelsior, MN 55364

THE END